PENGUIN BOOKS

FEARLESS NADIA

Dorothee Wenner is a freelance writer and film-maker based in Berlin. She also works as a curator for the Berlin International Film Festival. Her passion for Indian cinema started while researching for this book. Since then she has become a frequent visitor to Mumbai, working on various projects. She made a documentary on 'The Ladies Special' train in Mumbai, and has been co-curator for an exhibition on 'Bollywood–Indian cinema and Switzerland' in Zurich's Museum of Design. Her latest project is a multimedia exhibition on cultural transfer called 'Import/Export', which explores the mutual perception between India and Germany/Austria in times of globalization.

Rebecca Morrison studied modern languages at Oxford and lived in Berlin, Germany, for years, working as a translator and literary agent with a special focus on Indian literature. She is currently based in London.

Nadia, 1937

Fearless Nadia

The True Story of Bollywood's Original Stunt Queen

DOROTHEE WENNER

Translated from the German by Rebecca Morrison

PENGUIN BOOKS

An imprint of Penguin Random House

PENGUIN BOOKS

USA | Canada | UK | Ireland | Australia
New Zealand | India | South Africa | China | Singapore

Penguin Books is part of the Penguin Random House group of companies
whose addresses can be found at global.penguinrandomhouse.com

Published by Penguin Random House India Pvt. Ltd
4th Floor, Capital Tower 1, MG Road,
Gurugram 122 002, Haryana, India

Penguin
Random House
India

Originally published in German as *Zorros Blonde Schwester: das Leben der indischen Kinolegende Fearless Nadia* by Ullstein Buchverlage GmbH & Co. KG, Berlin 1999

First published in English by Penguin Books India 2005

10 9 8 7 6 5 4 3 2

For sale in the Indian Subcontinent only

Typeset in Sabon by S.R. Enterprises, New Delhi

ISBN 9780143032700

Printed at Manipal Technologies Limited, India

www.penguin.co.in

FSC www.fsc.org MIX Paper | Supporting responsible forestry FSC® C043100

This is a legitimate digitally printed version of the book and therefore might not have certain extra finishing on the cover.

Contents

FOREWORD TO THE INDIAN EDITION

It was a special moment for me when the original German version of this book was published. Yet, there was something missing: my Indian friends and supporters (especially Riyad Wadia and his family) were not able to read what I had written about Fearless Nadia. J.B.H. Wadia's daughter Haidee, who had married a German engineer and lived with her family near Stuttgart, was the only family member who could read the text. Haidee has passed away since then, and while reading the English translation of the book, I was acutely aware of the precious moments she, amongst so many others, had shared with me during the time of research. As this book is in part also a reflection of a certain time, we decided not to update the portraits and reflections of Nadia's former colleagues, who became protagonists next to the star herself. This decision was made when Riyad Wadia was still alive, as he was my friend and adviser. He passed away on 30 November 2003, leaving behind his grieving family and friends all over the world. Without Riyad's help, knowledge and wonderful ability to translate nuances of Indian culture to outsiders like me, this book would not have been written. I would like to dedicate the book to his memory.

Many thanks to all those who made the Indian edition of this book possible. First of all to Rebecca Morrison, the translator, for her sensitive work. To Riyad Wadia for some highly insightful additions. And to Penguin Books India for believing that a biography of one of Indian film history's greatest icons, written by a German, is worth being translated and published in India. I sincerely hope that readers will enjoy the recollections of a period of Indian film-making that was highly eventful, entertaining and thrilling.

December 2004 *Dorothee Wenner*

PROLOGUE: THE FIRST ENCOUNTER WITH NADIA

It began with a punch in the face delivered by a plump blonde in a scanty tiger-skin bodysuit to her moustachioed adversary. The cinema audience was enthralled by the tempestuous lady, and *Fearless—The Hunterwali Story* became the hot favourite at the 1994 Berlin Film Festival. The documentary reconstructed the incredible acting career of stunt legend Fearless Nadia, who in the mid-1930s had caused a real stir in Indian cinema. Sixty years later, the public at the Berlin Film Festival was dumbfounded and enthused to discover a radical feminist actress in Indian cinema history, one who wielded revolvers to the accompaniment of rousing music, then raced along the top of rushing trains, beat up men and played with lions. Nadia was smart, self-confident, and so funny into the bargain that it was well nigh impossible to distinguish between what was real in the life of the actress, and what belonged to the world of fiction according to oriental standards.

After the screening it transpired that the director was a great-nephew of Fearless Nadia. Riyad Wadia had dug deep into the family archive and created a wonderful memorial to his great-aunt who had faded into oblivion. I was not the only member in the audience to hang a photo of this actress over my desk after this cinema experience. Unofficial fan clubs sprang up. What was the secret of this woman's success, a woman who in the India of those days brought the public to wild, rapturous applause, and sixty years later in the West had what it took to become a feminist cult figure?

Four years after the Berlin premiere of his documentary film—Fearless Nadia had since died—Riyad Wadia granted me access in Bombay to enormous tin chests full of photos, screenplays, newspaper cuttings, receipts, studio plans and glass-plate negatives which contained parts of Fearless Nadia's story and that of her producers' studios. And he introduced me to the eccentric circles of stars and film buffs of Indian cinema in the 1930s and 1940s.

Fearless Nadia—it takes a short moment, but then the name sparks a happy gleam in the eyes of her now ageing fans. The men in particular start to smile conspiratorially, as though you had reminded them of a wild sin of youth. Some even make imaginary whips snap in the air at the thought of the cinema legend. Fearless Nadia was twenty-five years old when overnight she became a star with the film *Hunterwali*. The plump, athletic blonde girl stole the hearts, literally at a gallop, of the cinema-mad Indian public. Like Robin Hood she avenged the poor, beat up her enemies laughingly, rode like the devil and swung on chandeliers through the living rooms of the rich, sporting tight-fitting shorts. Mask and whip became the trademarks of this whirlwind woman who, as an Indian princess on-screen, led an extremely active double life. She boldly took liberties and embarked on a course no Indian actress had dared before—and all this with a smiling matter-of-factness.

In the 1930s and 1940s, Fearless Nadia was one of the top stars of Indian cinema. Yet, her films counted as cheap entertainment for the masses of uneducated factory workers and tonga drivers. Although this exceedingly wild, zestful woman with her laugh, her blonde mane and her rebellious sex appeal turned the heads of countless fans from Africa to the Far East, from Calcutta to Lahore, the rather snobbish intellectuals and respected film critics turned up their noses and ignored Fearless Nadia. This, however, didn't affect her popularity in any way.

Nadia's husband, erstwhile director and producer Homi Wadia, is now an eighty-eight-year-old gentleman with a full social diary. The first time I met him was at the horse races in Bombay, a place he suggested and one where he was absolutely at home. He appeared in an elegant Trevira Jersey suit, in the best of spirits, accompanied by his favourite niece Haidee, greeting people left, right and centre. This is a man people know in Bombay. The lift boy was enlightened too, and with a polite 'Thank you, Mr Wadia' slipped his tip out of sight. It was hot, the fans were whirring at full throttle, but of course it was the done thing to keep one's jacket on. In the white box, binoculars were placed at the ready and the programme studied. A waiter brought sweet peppermint tea and sandwiches. All around, one could see Bombay's high society mingling, the ladies showing off splendid saris that came wonderfully into their own against the oh-so-green lawns.

Afterwards, Homi Wadia invited me to his apartment which is decorated with numerous items of memorabilia. With this as a backdrop, Homi, quite the charmer and entertainer, recounted tales of Nadia, and the generous top-ups of the aperitif guaranteed the stories from the past were narrated to great effect. It wasn't hard to gather that the grand seigneur was able to look back on decades enviably rich in adventure and pleasures. With such a past, you age with dignity and elegance, and the repertoire of incredible anecdotes seem bottomless. He spoke willingly of his life with Nadia and the times of their shared major film successes.

Other 'stars of yesteryears' I met during my stay in Bombay also made a lasting impression: Babubhai Mistri, the 'man with the magic hands', eighty-two years old and an attraction himself—he still directs a weekly TV series on the life of Lord Krishna, noteworthy not only with a view to his age. Like his Wadia Movietone colleague, Babubhai Mistri enjoyed the wild nightlife in the Bombay film scene, naturally somewhat more intensely as a young man than today. In so doing, he smoked a great deal, leading one day to an operation for cancer of the larynx. Since then he has spoken a most mysterious language that can only be deciphered by the women who surround him, solicitously taking care of him, while his omnipresent director's assistant translates for the actors, business partners and visitors. When there is a certain professional secret that Babubhai Mistri does not wish to air, he uses his scratchy voice as the perfect veil. His living room, its walls decorated with impressive trophies and enormous Krishna statues, has the air of a temple and seems the appropriate place for remembering his work with Fearless Nadia.

Then there was Nadia's friend and former colleague, Pramila, of whom photos abound as the breathtakingly beautiful Miss India in 1947. As an actress she was deemed so sensual by the public of the time that the Indian censors once had twelve policemen escort her for a trial. The two actress friends were united not least by a cosmo-political element: 'There was as much mixed blood flowing in Nadia's veins as in mine; one of my grandmothers was a Russian Jew, the other one came from Lahore. With an American father, the grandfathers came respectively from Turkey and Baghdad. Nonetheless, deep inside both Nadia and I were Indian!'

***

Though largely disregarded in the West, more films are produced in India than in Hollywood—exported from Bombay into the so-called 'Third World'. In 'Bollywood', one of Fearless Nadia's relatives reveals, rumours spread quicker than in any other city in the world. As they gather speed, the stories are peppered with juicy details and dramatic climaxes. Premieres, scandals, huge profits, losses of millions, and murders lend wings to the narrative tempo. Film schedules are dictated by the stars alone who often work in five or more films at once and are worshipped like gods on earth. With their astronomical salaries, many of them lose sight of any reality, but that does not matter. The Indian public does not demand reality from cinema and its stars, but rather a dreamland into which one can escape when necessary. Whoever has the money goes to see their current favourite film over and over again, and many spend the same sum of money to keep abreast, through countless film magazines and fan rags, of the latest goings-on and the twists and turns of fate of the elect few in the 'Galaxy of Stars'.

Space is limited up there and the laws are tough. Hardly anyone lasts long. The actresses in particular have it hard, for, in India, women remain stars only as long as they are very young, very beautiful and unmarried. 'Married women are not suited to the life of the film studio,' Sibte Hasan Rizvi, a Bollywood producer with oiled hair, mirrored sunglasses, white suit and two mobile phones, explained to me. 'Bollywood is too much ablaze with the present to busy itself in the tidy European way of working through its own past.' Hits of the recent successful films blare out from the loudspeakers of street vendors. The melodies alone stick, everything else easily fades into oblivion. That made it all the more interesting and all the more difficult to research the biography of cinema legend Fearless Nadia.

It is clear that in the estimation of the people who mattered in the film business in those days—directors, producers, film critics—the story of the young actress was not the stuff of bright, flashing lights. For decades, Nadia remained an almost fairy-tale figure wrapped in the mist of mythology, a fog that until today has never completely lifted. Of all people, how did a blonde with European features succeed in becoming a celebrated stunt queen in popular Indian cinema?

Pursuing the fascinating life of Fearless Nadia provides insights into the life of cosmopolitan Bombay and the rich popular culture of a thoroughly cinema-obsessed country. Shortly after talkies took root in India, Nadia made her first film. They were the formative years of the so-called studio system in which films were made in often adventurous conditions. At that time, the film business did not revolve purely around money, and the movie-making pioneers around Nadia placed great emphasis on relaxing after hours in pleasure-seeking Bombay. Nadia's career came at a time when India was struggling for independence from the British colonial power. Using subversive methods, Fearless Nadia fought for freedom and also for women's rights in her films. Yet no one would have accused her films of any pedagogical flaw—on the contrary, Fearless Nadia was a shimmering mixture of action, eroticism and progressive ideas, this rare combination rendering her exemplary modern to this day.

1

THE EARLY YEARS

Mary Evans, 1915

Mary's father, Herbert Evans, was a Scotsman. Like both his elder brothers, he had joined the British army as a volunteer at the age of sixteen. While the elder brothers were posted to India, twenty-six-year-old Herbert landed in Australian Perth, a rather bleak provincial town in those days. The young man, not averse to the pleasures of life, suffered homesickness to such a degree that he seriously considered leaving the army and returning home. However, before this came to pass, during an exuberant night out, he got to know Margret—a strikingly merry Greek, and the focus of the evening with her Egyptian belly-dancing show. Herbert was not the only one to cast an eye in her direction, but he did so with serious intent. Margret made no secret of the fact that she was considered the black sheep of the family, contact with whom was forever severed. As a young girl she had opted against a bourgeois existence and finally run away with a touring theatre group to Australia as a dancer. Margret was very taken by the charming Herbert and shortly after their first meeting they decided to get married. Before long the couple wished for a child. Four miscarriages followed and the doctor advised against another pregnancy. However, on 8 January 1908, a warm Australian late summer day in Perth, Margret Evans gave birth to a healthy little girl. She was christened Mary Evans.

Mary was just four years old when her father's regiment was seconded to Bombay. The British army in India was preparing for a possible attack by Russia and so Herbert set sail with his regiment. Margret and Mary followed one week later on a passenger ship. From the beginning of the twentieth century, it had become routine for wives to accompany their husbands to far-off, foreign postings in the enormous empire. Yet, in army circles, the families were merely tolerated, and the moves were correspondingly strenuous when soldiers were relocated. In contrast to the luxury vessels in which the wives of high-ranking officers glided gently towards unknown lands, the cheap cargo ships on which the soldiers' wives travelled afforded no European frills. There was a bunk and food, but many people, often travelling alone, were driven to near panic by the stink and the coarse habits on board. Experienced traveller that she was, Margret took it in her stride better than many of her fellow passengers, particularly as her destination, Bombay, enjoyed the reputation of being more broad-minded about foreigners than any other town in India.

The voyage at sea lasted two weeks. Margret and Mary stepped shakily on to Bombay's newly built Ballard Pier. After her quiet life in Greece and rural Australia, the first impressions of Bombay were absolutely overwhelming. Enthroned, facing the pier, was the Taj Mahal Hotel, built in 1901, the epitome of oriental elegance, bang smack in the middle of an unsurpassable chaos comprising dock workers, strollers, inquisitive onlookers, merchants and wealthy tourists. Just as described by the American author Mark Twain who travelled to India around the same time:

> Bombay! A bewitching place, a bewildering place, an enchanting place—the Arabian Nights come again! It is a vast city; contains about a million inhabitants. Natives, they are, with a slight sprinkling of white people—not enough to have the slightest modifying effect upon the massed dark complexion of the public [...] There is a rank of noble great shade trees across the bay from the hotel, and under

> them sit groups of picturesque natives of both sexes; and the juggler in his turban is there with his snakes and his magic; and all day long the cabs and the multitudinous varieties of costumes flock by. It does not seem as if one could ever get tired of watching this moving show, this shining and shifting spectacle ...[1]

Yet for Mary and her mother, Bombay was not only fairy-tale-like oriental magic. Margret, who spoke a very Greek sort of English all her life, got to know the harsh everyday life of the city from their first day on, having to make do with very little money. Herbert had organized a small flat in the harbour district of Colaba, home to many families of the British army right up to India's independence. In contrast to the huge villas on the other side of town, the small flats of Colaba did not offer cool parks, high walls, or European luxury—that sort of environment was reserved for rich Europeans and Indian nobility. Mary spent her childhood in poor conditions, right in the middle of the wild bustle beside the harbour promenade. Her father came home only on weekends as his unit was stationed ten kilometres from the gates of the city on the island of Elephanta. Margret soon began part-time work as a seamstress in a textile factory, very glad to have found a family again in Herbert's brothers living in India.

The Civil War in the USA had transformed Bombay into a booming textile centre at the end of the nineteenth century as from then on the English no longer imported their cotton from the USA but rather from India. At the

[1] Twain, Mark, *Following the Equator—A Journey around the World*, Vol.II, New York and London: Harper & Brothers Publishers, 1899.

turn of the century, Bombay was experiencing systematic expansion into a metropolis of colonial trade and industry. The true cosmopolitan nature of Bombay, as distinct from other cities in India termed cosmopolitan, has its origins here: neither Delhi nor Calcutta nor Madras are as cosmopolitan, as Western, as modern. Not all that long before, Bombay had been an insignificant fishing settlement presented by the Portuguese as a wedding gift to the British in 1661 when Katherina of Braganza was married to King Charles II. The Portuguese name harks back to this story: 'Bom Bahia' the 'good harbour'. Until the end of the nineteenth century, this harbour remained relatively un-noteworthy, for at that time Bombay was still isolated, cut-off from the Indian mainland by the Western Ghats. It was only through the construction of the railway and the opening of the Suez Canal in 1869 that the town developed into the western gateway of the British empire in South Asia. Within the space of a few years, the town built upon seven marshy islands emerged as one of Asia's largest industrial centres.

This development was made possible by an almost inexhaustible reservoir of workers. What enticed the majority of the inhabitants was the traditionally tolerant policy of the governors who, from the end of the seventeenth century onwards, had created in Bombay a refuge for immigrants and the persecuted from all over India. The factories that shot up like mushrooms during the cotton boom were located in the centre of the city and the workers lived in mostly hellish conditions in the immediate vicinity of the noisy, smoke-belching halls. It wasn't until countless people fell prey to the bubonic plague at the turn of the century that the British along with the influential Indian industrialists gave substantial thought to town planning. Wide, sweeping streets were laid for better ventilation. The newer districts followed the British example of garden cities, and all kinds of impressive buildings in the Victorian style came up. Soon, Bombay was adorned with the proud title 'Urbs prima in India', the first city of India. It even moved one German traveller, usually rather finicky, by the name of Erwin Drinnenberg, to rapturous enthusiasm:

> Upon entering the city the eye rests upon streets lined with monumental buildings ... Spotless districts in the European mould with broad streets set in greenery. Splendid avenues and cultivated gardens. Generous squares with statues and well-tended subtropical vegetation. Parks, beach promenades, with an international globe-trotting public [...] Bombay, like no other city in India, has the distinctive characteristics of a tastefully fine culture ... [which] ably combine[s] the advantages of splendid nature with the generosity of a modern town lay-out. The wide beach-promenades with their broad sweep of palm-fringed horse-paths and vehicle-lanes that lead from Colaba to Malabar Hill, tracing the seething bay, is a worthy detail of the beauties of the city conditioned by nature.

For the European Evans family, the optimistic upbeat mood of the city must have taken on an unreal quality at the start of the First World War. Though with the onset of the war the delivery of chemical colours from Germany had stopped, thus putting the brakes on the city's economic boom to some extent, the war was taking place far, far away, on the other side of the world, and had only an indirect influence on life in Bombay. As those in Herbert's regiment reckoned with transferral to Europe, he worried, as did both his elder brothers, about the fate of the young family if they were left behind in India with no menfolk.

Even though Herbert Evans had dark premonitions about the future, he and his brothers came home more frequently in the time leading up to their actual departure, to party exuberantly. At these get-togethers, Mary learned polkas and Scottish dances from her father and her first Greek love songs from her mother. These family parties were to provide her with her final memories of her father. In 1915, Herbert Evans and his brothers fell in an offensive against German troops in Reims. Margret could barely conceal her despair from her daughter; she didn't know if she should stay in India at all. Since Mary had reached school-going age in the meantime, Margret decided to send her to the Catholic boarding school in Claire Road. Mary stayed there for six years and looked back on this time as an extremely happy one. Her mother laboriously attempted to scrape together the bare essentials for survival.

The British colonial rulers had, for the most part, left schooling to the missionaries, and there were thousands of so-called convent schools in India. They were attended primarily by British children whose parents weren't wealthy enough to have their offspring brought up in England, but there were also Indian Christians, Anglo-Indians, and, from 1900, Indian children of other religions were admitted as well. With the passing of time, the educational focus of the convent schools had shifted somewhat. When Mary went to school, rather than religious conversion, the conveying of Western values had taken centre stage. A generation was to be raised to be later drafted into the gargantuan apparatus of colonial administration. The Indian Christian pedagogue Malcolm Adiseshiah reminisces:

> One very important value was honesty, because the Hindu tradition doesn't pay much attention to being absolutely honest. One of the curious things my mother used to say was: 'Tell the truth like an Englishman.' And it was true that we never said 'no'. In Tamil, my language, if you say 'no' it is bad manners. So even though you mean 'no', you'll say 'yes'. Now this kind of thing, we learnt, is out. It was one of the things that the Christian institutions taught us.[2]

The Nuns' Favourite

Besides noble Western values, school was also the place where children like Mary had their first personal experiences with the ethical and religious hierarchies of the country. The English girls were consistently treated rather better than the others: 'One of my good friends at that time was a sweet south Indian girl, a Syrian Christian I think, and she was always getting into trouble even for things she never did. I was always considered to be English. However, Mummy was Greek and spoke English with a heavy Greek accent and I used to feel very embarrassed. In those days to belong to the establishment you had to be very pucca in your style of speech, dress, and manners. Not like today when people have no

[2] Masani, Zareer, *Indian Tales of the Raj*, London: BBC Books, 1987.

uniform value to go by. I guess you could say that I was never too sure as to where I belonged ... though I never thought of myself as un-Indian. Many people used to call me Anglo-Indian, even though I was not born in India.' Mary shared this cultural uncertainty with many Anglo-Indians growing up in Indian society. In lessons, the children's surroundings, the history of India, its culture, and most definitely its explosive present were completely ignored—this at a time when Mahatma Gandhi had breathed life into the Indian independence movement with the first of its spectacular campaigns. In Bombay's Christian schools the children sang every day in the church choir: 'Prima in Indis, Gateway of India/Door of the East with its face to the West/Here in Bombay we are living and learning/India our country, to give you our best.'

It was through the singing of songs like these that Mary's talent was discovered: the nuns became aware of her voice and gave their blonde favourite some solo parts in the church choir. Yet this special treatment didn't have quite the effect the nuns desired. Instead of concentrating on the content of the pious body of songs, Mary was one of the pupils who systematically widened the cracks in the wall between the boarding school and the outside world. And outside raged the roaring twenties: ballroom dancing, jazz, theatre and cinema provided Bombay with a hitherto unknown nightlife. Touring stars from Europe and the USA were fêted in the opera houses by enthusiastic audiences. Unlike the mothers of her classmates, Mary's mother didn't prevent her daughter from going to the cinema: 'I used to go to the flickers at every opportunity I got. When I came home on the weekends my mum used to give a few annas and I'd rush to the cinema hall with my friends. There were not many girls who were allowed to see films in those days. Many considered it to be a little cheap. But Mummy didn't have that view and so she willingly sent me. Of course I was only supposed to see pictures that were publicized as family fare. I once remember sneaking in to see Theda Bara's film *Salomé*. Mummy got very upset when she found out. You see, Theda Bara was called a vamp, and respectable girls were not supposed to behave like she did. It was all so funny.'

The result of all this was that Mary, to the horror of the nuns, wanted to become an actress.

At Uncle's of the Khyber Pass

Through her own experience of show business as a belly dancer, Margret contemplated Mary's choice of profession with scepticism. She knew all about the difficulties an artiste faces. In fact, the year 1922 brought so many problems that Margret was in no position to continue financing a life for herself and her now fourteen-year-old daughter in expensive Bombay. Despairingly, she looked around for a way out.

Since the British army at that time bothered little about the families of simple soldiers—particularly when the soldiers were long dead—the only remaining escape route were an 'uncle' and 'aunt' willing to take in Margret and Mary. The two women were related to these people only according to the unofficial version of the family history. In fact, the uncle was a close friend of Herbert's, worked as a vet in the British army, and longed for some company at his remote posting. So Mary left school prematurely in 1922 and travelled with her mother in the legendary

Frontier Mail to Peshawar, the border town at the Khyber Pass in today's Pakistan. For the British government, Mary was now one of the problem children, growing up all too far from schools, churches and tennis courts—severed from their influence.

Mary viewed it quite differently. It was the first journey she consciously experienced, one that took her farther from Bombay than ever before, where at the most she had been on excursions to the rather jungle-like forest land on the city's outskirts. She and her mother travelled for days in a north-westerly direction, through the dry Gujarat plains, along the twisting Indus, up into the mighty Hindu Kush mountains. Mary was enthralled: out of the train windows she saw countryside more impressive than anything she had seen of the world in cinemas. 'I'll never forget that journey! I had just turned fourteen and was stunned by the sights and the impressions en route. Until then I'd grown up a typical city girl, but now we were off to live in the country. I had no idea what was in store for me. The only thing Mummy kept repeating was that I might not be able to continue school as there wasn't a girls' school in the area. On top of that I had never met this uncle and his wife who we'd be living with, but she had promised to find some sort of work for Mummy in the army.'

Upon arrival they discovered that the uncle's base was about an hour away from Peshawar. He lived on a remote farm with horses, dogs, ducks and chickens. Nothing in this unsettled border country was as Mary knew it in Bombay: there were neither cinemas nor theatres, nor other places where a teenager, white and female to boot, could linger carefree. Among members of the army, the border town on the Kabul–Delhi route didn't rank as a popular post. It was, and still remains, a dangerous, uncontrollable area of great strategic importance, that recently grabbed headlines as an enormous refugee camp in the Afghanistan War. In India's turbulent history there has scarcely been an attack that has not started from this place. Even present-day travellers describe Peshawar as an extremely wild town in which there are as many firearm manufacturers as there are MacDonald's in other places. Even in the 1980s, according to one American traveller, the police, as a precaution against car theft, sometimes let the air out of tyres of all cars that happen to have stopped in the town.

In 1922, the year that Mary and Margret arrived at their new home, the Indian viceroy's wife Alice, countess of Reading, was travelling in the region with her husband, and reported to her family in England:

> They are a rough lot up here and shoot (as a man in hospital explained to me) like we use a handkerchief. Such a splendid race of men, very tall, as lithe as panthers, swarthy hair bobbed as the girls do at home, also locks plastered on their cheeks. They shoot members of their own family or anyone who happens to offend them or whose grandfather or great-grandfather offended them. One said yesterday [interpreted]: 'I shot him, I bore him a grudge but I don't know what for, it was a family grudge.' The hospitals here are crowded with men and even women and children with gunshot wounds in face, legs and arms, all from the same causes [...] At the Mission Hospital they have an enormous courtyard with beds all round open to the sky. The caravaners come in and are attended to there in

rows. One woman had her nose cut off because she was unfaithful! Squatting all over the floor are the relations all rolled up in old blankets, shawls, carpets and sacks. The marvel is that anyone recovers from an operation, but they all do, the air is so pure and lovely they don't seem to need water. The caravans come in just by the garden gate. All the camels huge and shaggy with their saddle bags full of stuff to exchange and barter. Mules with their owners astride, their bundles belching every colour of the rainbow.'[3]

Although Mary hadn't spent all her time in Bombay in elegant clubs and exaggeratedly English tea salons, her new home was a huge adventure, and she enjoyed the country life in a wildly romantic way. Her aunt did make a dedicated effort to familiarize Mary with household matters, from cooking to embroidery, but Mary soon found that she had learned quite enough of those things, and set to acquainting herself with her surroundings. 'Life in the cantonment was fairly primitive then. Older officers and numerous soldiers lived in the barracks. Wives and children were accommodated somewhere nearby. It was a really dangerous area; you could find yourself in the clutches of small-time throat slitters and crooks anywhere. Well, we of course longed for some sort of entertainment and created it ourselves. We organized dances, at which the army orchestra played, and people occasionally produced theatre plays. I always had to sing. My uncle had a good record collection, and I spent hours listening

[3] Butler, Iris, *The Viceroy's Wife: Letters of Alice, Countess of Reading, from India, 1921–25*, London: Hodder and Stoughton, 1969.

to the latest songs until I could sing them myself.' Immediately after arriving, Mary had learned how to ride—out of necessity, for horses were the sole dependable means of transport in the area. On her fifteenth birthday, she was given a chestnut-brown male pony called Tommy. This little horse, naturally, became Mary's best friend: 'My favourite ride with him led to a small river near the cantonment. The river was full of fish, and I spent entire afternoons there, fishing and playing. There was a flat piece of terrain there where the regiment practised, tent pegging and such like. When no one was around, I practised myself and tried to imitate the soldiers. Eventually I got to know some of the soldiers who taught me their tricks. Because my uncle was their subaltern they were always a little nervous, but they looked after me real well.' On one of those afternoons, Tommy pulled free from the tree to which Mary had tied him with the reins. For two whole despairing days there was no sign of him. Rather than comforting her, Mary's mother told her how irresponsible she was. 'I was just devastated. On the third day I went on foot to the little river where I normally rode Tommy. As I was sitting there, weeping, I felt something tickle my neck. I turned around, and there was Tommy! I kept on weeping, but now I cried with joy. He really was my best friend!'

Teenage Trouble

At an age when horses are a girl's best friend, it is well known that difficult problems also rear up. For Mary, it was her figure. She was overweight, and the fat stubbornly stuck to her, long past the puppy fat stage. The situation didn't change in spite of her constant exercise outdoors. When her first romance with a good-looking officer came to an end, Mary decided to do something to combat it. Yet at this point, as Mary, aged seventeen, was beginning to report on her early attempts to slim down in the unpublished family chronicles, an impenetrable curtain falls.

On 26 November 1926, Robert Jones was born, known from then on simply as Bobby. This boy went on to make a career as a hockey player in the Indian national league in the 1950s and is retired today, having worked in the service sector in Australia. It remains unclear who he really is. Sometimes he was called 'Mary's brother'; at other times he was introduced as her 'cousin' while in all probability he was her son. It wasn't until 1972 that Mary and her husband Homi Wadia officially adopted Bobby as their 'son'—and nothing further was discovered on the subject in her lifetime. According to Homi Wadia's version of events, Mary and Margret had journeyed to England at that time to look for work. Mary tried to get into drama school there too, but was advised otherwise: there was an abundance of pretty girls in England, and she shouldn't waste her life under the illusion that she could succeed. In England, they met acquaintances of Margret who were even poorer than the visitors from India, and, full of pity, Mary's mother declared herself willing to look after one of the many children. The English police officially approved this spontaneous adoption. Whatever may have been the truth, from 1926, Margret, Mary and Bobby formed a tight-knit family unit. And it was around that time that the resolute Greek decided that Mary must earn her own money, and that Peshawar was an unsuitable place. On short notice, a friend organized accommodation for Mary in Bombay and the Frontier Mail carried her back in May 1927.

As in Life, So in Film

Until this point, Mary had led a life reminiscent of the prologues of many of her films. The prologues serve to set the mood for the main action and enthral the audience in the first few minutes with a mostly very adventurous, fateful childhood episode. *Jungle Princess* (1942), for example, follows this pattern and tells the following story: a girl of about four embarks on a faraway voyage on board a ship with her father. She is a happy little soul, with a zest for life—a real gem, just like Mary as a child. Curiously, the girl in the film has blonde curls and very European characteristics while her father is unmistakably portrayed through his dress and accent as a north Indian businessman. The viewer learns nothing about the dead mother. Perhaps she could have been a European? Father and daughter are running away, from what or from whom remains a mystery. Yet, in spite of the mother's death, they try to look to the future with confidence. The father's briefcase helps them to do so, full as it is of money and valuable papers. Whoever is in possession of this briefcase can lay claim to entire streets in Bombay. While the father is describing to his daughter the prospects of their lovely new home, a mighty storm blows up. The waves pound the decks dramatically, and in a wild panic the sailors endeavour to save the vessel. But the force of nature is stronger, and the ship threatens to go down. The father and the noble sailors decide that the little girl shall have the only lifebuoy. With the best of wishes and warnings, the blonde is tied to it, along with the briefcase and her doll that are to accompany her on her watery journey. And then shc is off, her father waving after her, disappearing into the swell. By some miracle the girl survives and regains consciousness—with a dry little dress and perfect corkscrew curls—as the sun is rising the next day on a sandy beach in Africa. There she grows up as princess of the jungle, and echoes of her reputation as a brave ruler reach India where dwells a greedy uncle who wants to rob her of her rightful inheritance. The time of the shipwreck and the film's present day are linked by a caption that tells the viewer, in dramatic lettering stretching from the bottom left-hand corner to the upper right-hand corner, that twenty years have passed.

Following this pattern, in many of her later films severe blows are dealt by fate—a raging fire, the murder of the parents or the kidnapping of the screen daughter—which pave the way for the later turbulence in the heroine's life. The director of these films, Homi Wadia, explains that stories of this kind are still very popular with filmgoers today as they provide an immediate dramatic lead-in that touches the emotions. Furthermore, it is customary in Indian cinema to tailor the material to the star. This method is also used in Hollywood, in Arnold Schwarzenegger films for example. The bodybuilder from a village in Austria speaks more through his muscles than through lengthy monologues, and when he does say something his sentences sound only partially American. His Austrian accent isn't got rid of via dubbing, but is transformed into a characteristic of his customary screen identity.

A similar thing was true in Mary Evans's case. In spite of her very white skin, very blonde hair, blue eyes, and unusually powerful build, the audience accepted her as

Indian. The prologues before the story proper provide the necessary legend. As a cinema figure, Mary, going by the name of Nadia, isn't simply the young girl next door; she plays women with unusual, dramatic destinies. What happens to her in early childhood is so breathtaking that her appearance needn't be connected to a profane European origin. On the contrary, her appearance corresponds more visibly to her roles as ruler, as avenger, as rescuer in emergencies. That also explains incidentally why the 'child' Mary Evans in *Muqabala/The Duel* (1942), in which Mary has a double role, is played by a delightful child star with dark skin and black hair—Baby Madhuri, sister of heroine-to-be Meena Kumari. The credibility factor of a biological development of these two 'dark' girls into blonde sisters with European characteristics is not questioned as the two sisters take such contradictory paths after their early separation as is possible only in the realm of the action-packed film.

Falling Between All the Stools: The Bombay of Others

After four years in Peshawar, Mary Evans returned to Bombay and got to know other aspects of the metropolis. There was seething unrest in the city; the Indian independence movement, going from strength to strength, rendered the contours of the contrasts between Europeans and Indians more visible and tangible than ever before. While there was no official segregation policy, there was nonetheless a plethora of rules that determined everyday life and repeatedly made even the Indian upper strata painfully aware that they—just like the workers and farmers—were at best second-class citizens in their own country. In trains, for example, some carriages were reserved 'For Europeans Only' and it could lead to scandal if an English official at a social event danced first with an Indian woman and only afterwards with an English lady. It was a stock turn of phrase that the British underwent an enormous change, depending on where you got to know them—'to the East or to the West of the Suez Canal'.

Colonial racism was particularly perceptibly practised at the numerous clubs used by the British community as their most important social forum for relaxation, reading, playing cards, sport pursuits and business. Dorothy Ganapathy, the daughter of an Indian politician, recounts the famous anecdote of the founding of the first club in Bombay that became well known as a meeting place befitting upper-class Indians and Europeans. It sprung from the initiative of Lord Willingdon, the then governor of Bombay. The Englishman, famed for his liberalism,

> ... invited four or five Maharajas to the Yacht Club for dinner. When their cars drew up, they were not allowed to enter; so they were all outside. Lord Willingdon came down and said: 'Where are my guests? It's now coming on to nine o'clock.' And they said: 'Indians are not allowed.' So he came out and said: 'I'm sorry.' And he then and there wrote his resignation from the Yacht Club. He collected whatever food he could—he was governor after all—and they went to Government House and had dinner. And that day they sat down and decided to form a club. Lord Willingdon said: 'Yes, for Indians only.' And all the Maharajas, who gave a lot of money, said: 'No, we're not vindictive. It's

> for everybody.' And that's how it was called the Willingdon Club. It was the first club that Indians and Europeans could go to and mix.[4]

The colonial clubs are still today an extremely odd institution. Within their four walls, they enable foreigners to operate in an absurd microcosm that professes to being a complete society, a kind of ideal type of England in miniature. Renuka Ray, the Indian wife of a British officer, confirms that the wives of the colonial rulers in the 1920s and 1930s conducted their stays in this parallel British universe with almost grotesque perfection: 'I did go to the club, and I knew how to play tennis and bridge and all the rest of it. But I could not tolerate some of the things they started saying, and I used to have long and bitter discussions with them. Eventually, I decided it was better for me not to meet them too much, because they didn't like me ... British memsahibs in India—and there were certainly notable exceptions—were people who had little conception of what was happening in the country. They lived in a very closed circle, went to the club and probably played tennis and things ... How they could close their eyes, I don't know, but I used to marvel at it—how they didn't see what was in front of them, the misery of the people when the famines were on and things like that. When there was relief work to be done, I was interested, and I used to work in the districts. I remember that someone came to see me because I was an ICS officer's wife; and while she was there, people who had to be helped came round and there were others who were helping them. She saw this, and I told her that I thought she ought

[4] Masani, Zareer, *Indian Tales of the Raj*, London: BBC Books, 1987.

to take an interest. Her reply was: "Don't you think you might get some disease if you mix too much with these people?" They were so immersed in keeping everything hygienic and clean in their homes. Every day they changed all the *jharans* [dusters]. They always had their servants use gloves before they served at table and things like that which irritated me considerably.'

In the recollection of many Indians, it is the memsahibs, the British wives of the colonial rulers, who bear a greater responsibility for the intensification of everyday racism than the men. The explanation is fairly simple: the colonies had gradually turned into places where all the women who couldn't be married off at home were sent. They were either seen as too poor or too ugly or could no longer find a bridegroom due to an all-too-libertarian turn in their life. In the colonies, so went the unwritten rule, all these things weren't put under a magnifying glass; as long as the lady in question was white and English she would find a languishing bridegroom all right. Once they arrived, many of the women transmuted the doubtless often brutal form of deportation into aggression which they unleashed upon their Indian fellow citizens. One of the few Indian women who had access to the memsahib circles, Dorothy Ganapathy, remembers these women with understandable displeasure: 'They didn't come from very good families at all. They married for the sake of marrying, I suppose, and companionship. And they became very haughty. They had dozens of servants, though they never had one servant in England; and they thought everyone of us was servant class ... I remember once at a gathering, one Englishwoman turned to me and said: "Oh, what beautiful English you talk." I said: "Really? I'm surprised you acknowledge it.

After all, we educated Indians talk English all the time. Thank you for noticing, but it's not a compliment."'

As the daughter of a dead British soldier, Mary, upon her return to Bombay, fell between all the stools: her origins, her appearance, and her language placed her in the colonial upper set, yet her nature and certainly her lack of means rendered her an alien in the luxurious world in which embroidery, bridge, and the correct way of pouring tea were vital survival skills. Generally speaking, it was considered difficult to find a suitable match for children of British origin who had grown up in India. With her interrupted schooling, her now somewhat coarse manners and her fatherless, small family unit with no savings, Mary's chances on the marital market were slim. For all her desire for freedom, Mary, at least in the secret chambers of her heart, must have longed for a snug home in that comical world of tea parties, for a regular income, servants, and entertainment. Probably she was harbouring such hopes when she considered a position at the Army & Navy Store that a friend had brought to her attention. She applied—and got the job.

Army & Navy was the first department store in the country, a splendid Victorian building offering the latest in consumer and luxury goods on its five floors, intending to make the stay in the colonies bearable for the British. Based on the model of large department stores like Macy's or the German Wertheim, Army & Navy was the top address in the Orient where you could find simply everything, from expensive toys to French perfumes to exclusive household goods—the Wedgewood counter was directly next to that of Chippendales. For the Europeans in the colonies it was viewed a particular challenge to remain up-to-date and not lag behind in the backwoods of fashion. No wonder then that shopping sprees in Army & Navy became social happenings, drawn out as long as possible with tea breaks on the various floors. An incidental result of the casual presence of high society was that the store became a kind of marriage market for the shop assistants who, due to their social status, were excluded from the exclusive inner circle of the clubs.

It was here, for example, that Rosemary Almeida, one of Mary's Anglo-Indian colleagues, got to know her husband-to-be, a British officer. 'For girls like us it was a unique opportunity to meet people from better society.' For Mary, however, the position in the cosmetics department was first and foremost an enormous challenge. Through her years in Peshawar she had lost all connection to urban life. She simply didn't know what the done thing was, how to move, what to wear, and what one talked about. But she soon realized that the boy-like behaviour she had grown used to among the rough soldier circles in Peshawar was not the norm here. Her colleagues accepted the wallflower and did their best to turn her into one of them, taking her along to jazz concerts and dances dressed in the right attire. One of the young ladies also urged Mary to do something about her large physique, to take up sport. But all their attempts were only moderately successful at best, for the acquaintances that Mary made in the department store and at the sports club were men who left Bombay after a brief sojourn. Frustrated by the glittering superficiality and through the necessity of developing a long-term perspective for her small family, Mary applied for a job as a secretary in a law firm. She got it and secured her position by doing a crash course in stenography. Yet scarcely a year in the office had gone by when Mary began to feel bored to death.

From Mary Emerges Nadia

The turnaround came in the form of an advert in the *Times of India.* A Russian ballerina by the name of Madame Astrova was looking for new students for her dance school. Mary, who from childhood had been a keen dancer, applied immediately. Dance school, she thought, would provide the ideal chance to mix pleasure with practicality: shed fat while having fun. Madame Astrova was an industrious, energetic lady of advanced years, who, like many of her Russian colleagues, had moved abroad in the aftermath of the turmoil of the October Revolution. The avant-garde artistes in particular felt the magnetic pull of India with its multifaceted dance tradition.

Ever since Isadora Duncan appeared in a Greek tunic and bare legs, specialists had been debating the folkloristic elements of classical ballet. The Moscow choreographer Michel Fokine, who had choreographed a performance of *Scheherazade* with India-inspired costumes, entered into a verbal duel with American expressionist dancer Martha Graham, recorded by Fokine in his memoirs. In a New York lecture, Martha Graham had described classical ballet as 'dreadful', whereupon Fokine asked her, despite her obvious reluctance to discuss with those of a different opinion, 'Why is ballet dreadful?' After he had forcefully repeated the question, Miss Graham went into the fifth position, giving the impression that this was most typical for ballet. 'How can Greek dances be danced like this?' was her poser. Fokine retorted, 'You know very little about ballet. You seem unaware that there are a whole number of ballets where the fifth position does not occur, ballets that are based upon singularly natural movements, along the most pure lines of Greek style. You criticize ballet without knowing it.'

Fokine's contemporary, the Russian choreographer Fyodor Lapuchov, experimented with mixed forms, both in theory and in practice:

> Let us take an example: *Bajadere*. What is Indian about that ballet? What Indian dances are these? I don't even want to think of the ridiculous hairstyles of the two ballerinas who performed the rival scene. The very concept of that scene was wrong. Raja's daughter calls the temple dancer to her and squabbles over the bridegroom. Ballet fans were enthusiastic because of their absolutely identical hairstyles, these 'page-boy' cuts. In the jealousy scene you saw two active members of the bourgeoisie, two mannequins or what have you, but certainly not two island inhabitants. What is to be done? Do you turn your back on a ballet where no real Indian resides? But that would mean losing a significant work of art, the silhouette from *Bajadere*.[5]

In India, the ideological chasms between different ballet schools could be more easily crossed. Ever since the famous Russian ballerina Anna Pavlova had, as a dying swan, ignited the enthusiasm of the Indian audience in the early 1920s, European and American ballet offerings had been part of the regular cultural programme, not just in Bombay,

[5] Wolgina, Lydia and Ulrich Pietzsch, *Die Welt des Tanzes in Selbstzeugnissen: 20. Jahrhundert*, Berlin: Henschelverlag, 1977.

although in the colonies fashionable expressionist dancing was interpreted in original ways—for example, Martha Graham's resounding success in Rangoon was thanks to the fact that local newspapers announced her as 'an elephant running amok'—and local dance studios had recently started working on East–West synthesis of dance. It was Rabindranath Tagore who initiated this.

In 1926, Tagore put his whole authority as poet, philosopher, director, and cultural politician on the line by propagating the play within a dance *Natir Puja*—with sweeping success. It was the first time that traditional temple dances were performed on the stage outside their religious context. Thanks to Tagore, young Manipuri dancers could be seen on stage. He succeeded in breathing secular life back into the art of Indian dance and created a real trend. Like the Soviet Union, the progressive powers in India began to unearth the treasures of their own folklore art, and develop it systematically. Because the so-called folklore ballet was suddenly equated with nationalism and even anti-imperialism, the dance schools in the cities soon offered not only foxtrot and charleston, but also Manipuri, Kathak and Keralan dances. Europeans like the free dancer Hilde Holger, born in Berlin in 1905, encouraged this tendency: 'I told them [the students]: "You have a wonderful tradition in Indian dance. You don't have to imitate classical European ballet. Return to your dance and expand upon it." I also did free dance with them, in doing so taking their lead and choosing things that are understood the world over, for example water, fire, earth. This very much appealed to them.' Like Madame Astrova, Hilde Holger had set up a dance studio in Bombay. Yet the pioneering success of Tagore's folklore ballet was still a long way from making dance studios respected institutions: 'When I first opened my studio, only men came, which I couldn't understand at all at first. They thought it was a brothel. They wouldn't believe it was a dance school. I said to them: "There's nothing to see here." My European friends enlightened me. On their advice I attached something additional to the sign, which now read "For Ladies Only", and the men stayed away, thank God.'

In contrast to Hilde Holger, Madame Astrova was still a teacher of the old school: she demanded the greatest discipline and loyalty, but to counter this also offered the students a close Russian solidarity. For Mary, who brought a quite considerable barrage of cultural influences with her for her age, Madame Astrova was the ideal teacher. After some teething difficulties, her stage talent developed remarkably. Both Madame Astrova and the other students were surprised, for Mary was hardly nymph-like. The grace with which she comported herself was unusual and spectacular. Mary herself found greater and greater pleasure in her lessons, which she had initially viewed as a hobby. When Madame Astrova, inspired by the successes of other dance schools, set to work on a tour programme, Mary resigned from the bleak secretarial job in the autumn of 1930 to participate in the tour.

In the meantime, Margret also returned to Bombay, with Bobby. Supportive of Mary's ambition, she was prepared at once to continue looking after Bobby and to let Mary move on. But there was still one thing to be done. Like many Indians, Mary, before reaching the decision on giving up her job, had gone to see a fortune teller. The Armenian lady laid the tarot cards for Mary and foretold that an extremely successful career lay ahead, but she also prophesied unhappiness in her private life. As a precaution, the Armenian suggested that Mary take on a stage name. After intensive questioning of the cards, they looked for a name beginning with 'N' and with five letters. Mary's fascination with Russian names led her to the idea of calling herself NADIA from that day on. A suggestion that Madame Astrova accepted immediately, for Nadia had a much more exotic ring to it than Mary.

The Chorus Girl Dances Her Way to the Top

The tour took Madame Astrova's troupe through the length and breadth of India: they danced for soldiers at military bases, on the open-air stages of villages and small towns, and also for maharajas in numerous Indian palaces. In her memoirs, Hilde Holger describes her tour experiences which were at times very similar to that of Madame Astrova and her troupe. About one performance at the court of the princess of Bhopal, Hilde Holger had this to say: 'Just as you imagine *One Thousand and One Nights*. But the audience consisted of men. The women were only permitted to watch through latticed windows. The piano that had been transported over seventy miles was in such a state of disrepair that after hitting each note, the pianist had to prise the key back out.' At the nawab of Hyderabad's court she had, amazingly enough, exactly the same experience as Martha Graham's sister Geordie on her Asian tour several years earlier: 'While they were dancing on the stage the nawab got down from his elevated throne, mingled with the dancers on stage, and touched the material of their tunics as they danced on. At the end of the performance he shook everyone's hand and indicated that his bodyguards should follow him; they bore a golden box encrusted with emeralds and rubies. He was the richest man in the world at that time. Geordie told me how full of anticipation they all were for the gift that he would bestow to each individual. The box was opened ceremoniously, and the first gift proffered: an orange.'

Nadia doing the ballet, 1932

Madame Astrova and her troupe probably encountered similar setbacks. The eternal lack of money and the tiring life on the road rendered immensely attractive the offers of interested soldiers and sailors to marry this or that dancer and remove her from the stage. Just as a good twenty years ago, Nadia's mother had married Herbert Evans, so too more and more dancers remained behind with their suitors after performances. Madame Astrova's troupe melted like ice in the sun. Nadia recognized in her pragmatic way the advantages of the situation. At the start of the tour she was dancing in the chorus only. Now, she asked Madame Astrova's permission to choreograph her own solo piece. As the delicate aesthetics of the original programme had gradually evaporated to conform to the taste of the audience, Nadia was eventually permitted to perform her solo gypsy dance, in which she revealed, among other things, her mastering of the cartwheel and the splits. The act was such a hit that Madame Astrova soon made Nadia the star of the show: there followed even more acrobatic numbers, later even song-and-dance pieces. The success brought new impetus to the group, yet this was to be short-lived.

In New Delhi, an argument arose between the resolute Russian and Nadia. Nadia felt—having been promoted to star—underpaid and exploited, yet the strict boss refused a salary rise. Drained by two strenuous years on tour with life on trains, cheap guest houses and all too many performances, Nadia didn't want to go on. She left the troupe and her teacher to try her luck alone.

In the Ring and in Front of the Screen

Nadia found the courage necessary for this step to independence as she had already made a name for herself in theatre circles. By chance, at this time the famous Zarko Circus was performing in Delhi as part of their Asian tour. A femalc variety performer fitted well with their programme, and Nadia was to entertain the audience during set changes. After three weeks of training, her first performance was scheduled. Nadia had gathered sufficient stage experience through her solo numbers to master this task to general satisfaction. But when the circus director fell sick and Nadia was asked to take over his place in the ring, it was to prove too much for the twenty-four-year-old. She rehearsed a number of times, found herself unsuited to this role, and left the circus very soon afterwards. 'I didn't like the circus, the work was too much for me,' was her appraisal of the intermezzo. She stayed in New Delhi and tried out a new business idea: she turned to the management of the Globe Film Theatre, a chain of cinemas in locations scattered throughout the country.

She negotiated her first contract and spent a few weeks in the city. The talkies hadn't yet reached India, and so there were little cinema orchestras everywhere. Supported by this musical accompaniment, Nadia wanted to perform little vaudeville sketches on the stage before the main film to draw in a larger crowd. Soon, however, she got to know a new Russian–German dance troupe specializing in gypsy dance, and she joined up. Then it was off on tour again. Nadia and her new troupe performed more and more frequently in cinemas and discovered a niche. Gradually, the talkies were beginning to dominate the big screen but it would be some years before the studios could cater for the demand in multilingual India, especially as all cinemas were not sufficiently equipped.

As long as silent movies were still shown in provincial places, Nadia and her colleagues offered a repertoire of off-screen noises and songs as a temporary solution for the last silent movies. These performances weren't professionally prepared by any stretch of imagination, and were largely exercises in ingenious improvisation. The process was made all the more difficult as Nadia barely understood what she was saying and singing. Unavoidably, things would go awry as in the performance of the film *Shirin Farhad*. As the heroine began to die, Nadia was supposed to accompany the scene with a very sad song. But, not for the first time, she had started the swansong more from a sense of intuition and faith in her good luck, discovering in the meantime that things weren't quite what she had thought. She sang and sang until she grew hoarse, but still the heroine wouldn't die. The audience was creased up with laughter by the time Nadia finally gave up. Her sense of humour rescued her from disgrace at such times, and often helped her out otherwise in times of difficulty.

Lone female travellers, especially Europeans, were very exotic apparitions in India in those years. Despite this, from the travelogues and diaries of these adventurous ladies, one gets the impression that it really wasn't all that problematic to travel around the country as a single female. Beyond the towns and the colonial enclaves there quite simply weren't any conventions yet that dictated the behaviour of journeying white women. For example, the writer Emma Roberts and the energetic adventurer Fanny Parkes travelled with great curiosity, free of prejudice. They attempted to learn Indian languages, spent weeks in various domiciles for women where they enjoyed themselves, taking sitar lessons, researching the biographies of thieves, and being taught the details of elephant training. Almost all facets of the Indian everyday seemed worthy of close study to both these women, and the dangers lurking at the corners did not seem to merit the slightest attention.

A similar form of psychological blocking, which generally isn't bad self-protection while travelling, was adopted by Nadia. Yet, little is known about what she otherwise experienced during that four-year-long journey—where she performed, where she felt comfortable, when she felt tired perhaps, drained and alone. According to the unwritten rules of colonial society, a travelling performer roving through India was synonymous with a sinful, loose life, an existence beyond etiquette. Understandably, even later on she preferred to drop mere hints when talking about this very turbulent chapter of her life. An example that proves that her life on the road was endangered on occasion is the episode in the town of Quetta where Nadia had performed in a hotel. Only hours after her departure, a violent earthquake destroyed the entire town, and in all probability Nadia would have been beneath the debris of the hotel had fate not had something better in store for her. As regards dangers other than natural catastrophes, Homi Wadia effortlessly produces a telling allegory: 'Nadia went from village to village from north to south with a couple of costumes and a gramophone player. During her travels, she often lived in dark bungalows that were lonely and far from other houses. Most of the time it was very hot, and the men warned her: "Just don't sleep outside whatever you do!" "No, no," she said—and did exactly that! She was very brave; she was a soldier's daughter after all. And besides that, there were stray dogs all over the place that Nadia made friends with, giving them something to eat, and so the dogs stayed with her. She loved all animals, especially dogs, and wherever she was, they slept nearby and kept watch over her.'

Nadia zigzagged the country with her colourful programme of dance, song, cabaret, and off-stage imitation, until she finally reached Lahore. She started working for a cinema owner there, who felt that her original and often very funny acts were wasted behind the screen or as interval-fillers. He recommended an address in Bombay to her: friends of his, the Wadia brothers, who had a film studio. She should try her luck as an actress there.

2

FILM PIONEERS

2
FILM PIONEERS

Hunterwali, 1935

By 1934, auditions were nothing new for Nadia. After the break with Madame Astrova, she had sought out possibilities for performing with theatre and cinema owners on her own steam. To these meetings she always took her brown photo album that still exists today. Each page shows Nadia posing in various guises: saucy as a vaudeville dancer or a fiery gypsy woman, as a Greek nymph or an athletic free dancer in a scanty bathing costume. Yet, in spite of her considerable stage experience, illustrated impressively in the photo album, Nadia by no means had insider studio know-how at her fingertips. She knew neither the Wadias nor the films they had produced. The two Wadia brothers, Homi and Jamshed (known to everyone as JBH) were among ten producers in Bombay with good prospects of mastering the complicated transitional phase from silent movies to sound films without going bankrupt in the process. Eruch Kanga, the befriended cinema owner from Lahore, had waxed lyrical about Nadia's capabilities to the two film pioneers and had set up an appointment.

Nadia was so nervous that even decades later she could recall this momentous meeting down to the last detail. 'I'd told friends I was trying out for work at Wadia Movietone and they told me it was a film production company with a good reputation. Well, when the day came I took the tram from Wellington Mews in Colaba, not far from my home at that time, and rode out to Parel where the studio was. Parel was a very posh neighbourhood and the studio was located right next to the house of the governor of Bombay. In those days, the area was on the edge of town, and behind the studio were lots of paddy fields, and you could look over to Antop Hill and out to Borivili—no skyscrapers blocking the view. I remember I had treated myself to a sweet, sky-blue dress for the interview, along with a pretty little hat complete with sunflowers. When I alighted from the tram, Mr Kanga was there waiting for me in his red Chrysler and we drove through the wrought-iron studio gates together. I had rather anticipated some sort of tin shed structures as I had seen these in Imperial Studios where I had sometimes watched filming in the silent-movie days. But suddenly we were driving up to a grand villa! The whole atmosphere led me to prepare myself for a meeting with some respectable elderly gentlemen. As we entered the lobby all I could see were some actors hanging around dressed as monkeys. It was quite funny.'

But Nadia was professional enough not to be further distracted by curiosities on the way to the head office and thus she swept past her later director and husband in a ladylike manner—she didn't even notice the rather weedy figure in the corridor! However, J.B.H. Wadia corresponded rather more to Nadia's picture of a studio boss: older to his brother Homi by ten years, JBH sported an impressive pair of intellectual glasses and received Nadia as he continued chain-smoking behind his desk. The horror in his expression at her entry couldn't have escaped Nadia—his friend Kanga apparently hadn't prepared him for such a white, such a blonde and such a large woman. JBH later admitted that at first he thought Kanga was playing a trick on him. To salvage the embarrassing situation, Nadia remarked confidently that she was really rather famous in the world of theatre. JBH responded coolly that he had never heard of her. 'To which I said that until now I hadn't heard of him either! He then laughed a lot and I think he decided to hire me because of that.' At any rate, after the somewhat brusque introduction, the interview proper went rather well, during which Nadia presented her brown photo album and listed off her talents: she could swim, ride a horse, dance, she was very athletic, of a gymnastic disposition, no less, and could do the splits.

For an Indian actress in those days, these were unusual qualities. Furthermore, it didn't escape JBH's producer's eye that Nadia had a majestic figure, beautiful teeth which gleamed in her mouth, and piercing blue eyes framed by corn-blonde hair. When he inquired about her competence in languages, things got tricky. Nadia could speak Greek but didn't understand any of the Indian languages, neither Hindi or Urdu nor Marathi or Gujarati. JBH sent for his brother—he didn't want to make the decision about employing the future actress on his own. Homi felt snubbed at the first official confrontation: 'She laughed herself blue in the face when she saw me! "What, this man decides such matters?" she asked my brother!'

Somehow, all four characters must have found each other very curious that day, curious enough at the same time not to go their separate ways immediately. So JBH offered Nadia a starting salary of sixty rupees a week. His brother thought him crazy for this, but accepted the decision. Nadia's first task was to take home a Hindustani scene and learn it by heart. A week later she was to return and Homi would do the test shots. 'I was still unsure after this interview, but sixty rupees a week wasn't a bad start and I wanted to come and settle in Bombay as I was tired of travelling!'

Nadia, therefore, took great pains and practised the Hindustani text at home—yet the results were shattering. 'A disaster!' was Homi Wadia's verdict. Her utterly wooden way of declaiming was dreadful. Added to that was her grotesque accent. 'It was a pure joke.' But Nadia had other talents that simply fitted too well to the Wadia brothers' history. Swimming, horse riding, acrobatics—the stuff of stunt films!

A Rebel Lawyer and Other Film Pioneers

Even as a ten-year-old schoolboy, J.B.H. Wadia, who was born in Surat in 1901, was hooked to movies. Every weekend found him drifting from one cinema to the next with two friends. If they took the cheapest seats right in front of the screen, their pocket money would stretch to two or three films a day. Those were the days in India when complaints about too few films and far too few cinemas in the country were unabated. Ever since the first movie was shown in 1896, Indians had fallen head over heels for the miracle of the century, the cinema. This immense demand didn't escape the notice of the European and American film distributors and thus, in the silent-movie era, almost everything produced in Italy, France, Russia, Japan, Germany and the USA was shipped to India. J.B.H. Wadia and his friends weren't too concerned by the lack of Indian films; they preferred American Westerns and weekly action serials anyway: 'All that I had to do now was to keep [my eyes] open in the cinema house and identify myself with the daredevil heroes [...] such as Harry 'Cheyenne' Carey (who was my prime favourite), Tom Mix, William S. Hart, Francis Ford, Eddie Polo [...] The cinema became my cherished dream world.'[6]

As a rule, these serials consisted of fifteen episodes, and from the opening minute to the last the audience was guaranteed mad stunts with breathtaking excitement, wild fights and shootouts, rounded off with a cliffhanger in the closing seconds. What was later to become Hitchcock's trademark was used by the producers of early silent movies as a lure to keep the audience in anticipation a week long.

[6] Wadia, J.B.H., *Those Were the Days*, Bombay.

The stampede for entrance tickets became the athletic prelude to what the screen heroes would continue in incomparably dangerous form. JBH and his two friends had developed an ingenious system to make their way to the front of the ticket booth in the tumult. The first one, with the money, stood at a safe distance to evade the numerous pickpockets. The second scrambled through the crowd until he reached the booth. 'Sometimes he would frog jump over the shoulders of others verily like a monkey.' The first one in the meantime got closer in his turn to his pal at the booth so as to hand over the carefully counted coins for three tickets at the right moment. 'My job was to run up to the main door of the third class and manage to push my way forward by hook or by crook [...] The doors would be immediately thrown open after the entire audience of the previous show had gone out ... There would be a veritable stampede of cine goers in the auditorium [...] Then I would try to secure the best seats possible on the wooden benches by laying myself prostrate on one of them. This was the accepted technique for reservation of seats in those days [...] As a result, for about the first half minute or so, one would witness the strange spectacle of the first batch of cine goers all lying supine and glued to their respective areas, motionless like so many corpses. It was funny to see all those "corpses" strewn out before the screening began! [...] We had to be through with the whole circus before the swift and fierce ticket collectors did their rounds. Of course, in the elegant cinemas with their "first class balconies" it was quite a different story, where even the doormen acted as though they were film stars! They held spray cans and sprinkled the seats so generously with rosewater that countless viewers reacted as though they had been smoking hashish and fell back into their chairs in a trance.'

For all his love of cinema, it was only after a long, academic detour that J.B.H. Wadia decided to enter the film business himself. He had studied literature and law, and his family believed him to be on the right path to a bourgeois existence at the Indian Central Bank. They hadn't the faintest idea about his hobby. He had started writing his own screenplays, which he submitted—in vain—to the large studios for possible filming. Then, in 1926, he came across an advertisement in the Gujarat weekly paper *Mouj Majah*: a cameraman from the famous Kohinoor Studios was seeking a financial partner for a feature film! J.B.H. Wadia contacted him straightaway, and promptly, this 'partner with no previous experience' had a foot in the door. As a passionate film buff, he had a vast knowledge of film theory at his fingertips, but no idea about the practicalities of film production, of camera technology and sequence of motion. The cinema-enthused lawyer henceforth used every free minute to watch the then star director, Homi Master, at work.

The higgledy-piggledy hustle and bustle struck him as extremely chaotic: whenever the clouds in the sky vanished, frantic activity ensued. Everyone went to their positions, faces were powdered afresh, the cameras honed to focus. Some coolies were hurriedly brought in as extras from the nearby station and shooed this way and that. Technicians yelled at actors who had chosen an inopportune moment for a tea break, the artists had forgotten to give the final lick of paint to the all-important backdrop for the next shot, once again someone had spat out red betel nut juice on the floor of the studio palace. The chaos, however, didn't confine itself to the technical side of film production.

Once JBH was witness to tempestuous arguments between Homi Master and his lead actor. The two of them yelled at one another until the actor refused to act any more. In the heat of the moment, Homi Master decided to alter the screenplay. Briefly, a certain panic erupted, but the director remained calm and decreed that the studio mutt be brought to him. The dog, according to the new screen directions, would from this scene adopt the role of the hero because a sorcerer had magically brought about this transformation. The heroine was horrified and burst into tears when suddenly instead of kissing the handsome charmer she had to kiss the dog. Filming continued with this 'alternative cast' until the original hero, anxious about his future career, declared that he was ready to join in again. Homi Master had the dog transformed back by magic—and in the finished film the whole episode provides an amusing escapade which fits logically to the story and was applauded enthusiastically by the audience.

The Track to Producer's Sweet Success

Film-making in those days called for a talent for improvisation, and precisely this ability was required above all others by the new producer J.B.H. Wadia in his first film. His own screenplay *Vasant Leela* was selected as the material and in spite of financial uncertainties five partners—the cameraman, G.S. Devare, the only one among them with a certain professional experience at his disposal—set to the preparations with enthusiasm. Until one of the quintet, Navnitrai Hargovandas Shah, a financier with Selznick-inspired dreams, died of sudden heart failure. His death crippled further work and Solomon Samson, an advocate and aspiring actor, decided he was no longer interested in the project. Shortly afterwards, an argument arose among the remaining three partners and Indulal Yagnik departed from the dream world of cinema to hit the headlines several months later as the enfant terrible of the Marxist Worker's Movement in Amritsar. J.B.H. Wadia began contemplating the end of his brief dalliance with the film business, but the remaining partner, Devare, was an experienced cameraman, and like the young lawyer wanted to continue come hell or high water. Indeed, a few weeks later the two partners found a rich businessman who secured a loan for them. And now the moment had come for JBH to have to explain to his family that he was giving up his promising career as a lawyer to make his name as an absolute beginner in the milieu spurned by 'respectable' society. The ensuing crisis went on for weeks—until his mother granted her son one year to try his fortune. If he didn't succeed in keeping a tight rein on his senses and the siren-like actresses at bay, she was authorized to haul in her rebel son.

J.B.H. Wadia with film crew, 1934

After dragging on for several nerve-racking months, *Vasant Leela* was finished, but the shaky melodrama, with JBH as screenwriter, director's assistant and PR manager, sank into oblivion not long after its premiere on 29 September 1928. Although the film earned out its production costs, no one dared risk a further project in partnership with J.B.H. Wadia for the next two years. It took months for him to acknowledge that *Vasant Leela* hadn't failed because of the limited intelligence of its audience. His highflying plans shrunk to a petty bourgeois format. JBH shifted to providing a post-production service: going by the name of Wadia Film Exchange, a small laboratory was developed, combined with a cutting room and a slowly prospering film distribution network. The new profession involved intensive work but JBH could depend on one industrious, responsible helper. His brother Homi may still have been at school, but he was drawn to the studio complex every afternoon. And not long after, Homi—on the heels of renewed family quarrels—joined the business as a junior partner.

At almost the same time, the first sound film was produced in India in 1931, directed by Ardeshir Irani and entitled *Alam Ara*. The large studios found themselves compelled to acquire the expensive new equipment and to look out for scripts that would work in this revolutionary medium. Popular theatre plays began to be filmed but the actors had difficulty in speaking at the right volume into the heavy inflexible microphones. That rendered the first films so wooden and awkward that the smaller producers continued to focus on the action-packed, quickly shot stunt films of the silent-movie era. Furthermore, in the rural areas there were still a lot of cinemas that could not afford the conversion to sound film projectors.

JBH and Homi also believed in a future coexistence of silent and sound films. Since their laboratory and film distribution were gleaning small profits, JBH suggested to his younger brother that they film an Indian pendant to Douglas Fairbanks's *The Mark of Zorro*. The script lay ready in the drawer and Homi was enthusiastic about the idea. In the junk storeroom of Kohinoor Studios, they found an ancient camera, 'the oil can', which they purchased for 500 rupees. Homi looked for a lead actor and finally asked the athletic Yeshwant Dave to an audition. This consisted of gymnastic exercises for the most part. He showed the Wadia brothers how elegantly he could execute the forward roll from the most improbable starting positions and how far he could jump. He was given the lead on the spot, and JBH handed the directorial reins to Homi. *Thunderbolt* was filmed in ten days—in the open air, with a minimum of props and equipment. On the day of the premiere, it was pouring; Homi and JBH arrived at the cinema soaked through, the film canisters tucked beneath their arms. They had taken the tram, still a world away from being able to afford a car. The selected cinema wasn't one of the most elegant in town, the corrugated tin roof leaked and the audience had to sit beneath open umbrellas. That didn't dampen the enthusiasm, though: the film was a success and played until the copy could no longer be run through the projector. For financial reasons, the Wadia brothers had decided to film on good value positive material—a method that bestowed, as a rule, a short lifespan to films as there was no negative from which new copies could be made.

Thunderbolt brought in enough money for the next production—and the service business, Wadia Film Exchange, was shut down. The brothers dedicated themselves completely to producing films. Their next project *Toofan Mail* was a railway thriller, an Indian variation on the American Helen Holmes series. The young producer JBH wrote the screenplay and himself directed. Homi worked as cameraman in the *Toofan Mail* production which became more of an adventure than the finished film. The brothers had decided to film exclusively at original locations, but were of the opinion that a general filming permit would suffice. When Homi secured the cheap replacement camera to the tracks for the spectacular 'train travels over the heroes' heads' shot, he almost brought the oncoming train to an emergency stop, and the two brothers were put under short-term arrest. They talked their way out and even managed to get the stationmaster to allow them to film in the engine itself the next day. The condition was, however, that JBH would simultaneously be stoker and extra in the engine as space was limited.

With *Toofan Mail*, the brothers made a name for themselves as experts in stunt films. Established in 1933, the company name—Wadia Movietone—became synonymous with action-packed entertainment. Meanwhile, JBH and Homi Wadia had taken the extremely witty film distributor Munchesar B. Billimoria on board with them as a business partner. His reputation preceded him—an unerring nose for public taste, and a knack for investing his not too sumptuously large capital in the right projects.

The Mark of Zorro

It was Billimoria who encouraged JBH, in the wake of thc swiftly produced stunt films, to dare a return to serious material, as at the beginning of his career. The thrillers may have brought good box office returns, but were not taken seriously at all by the strata of society to which the Wadias belonged. Following the premiere of a new Wadia stunt film, Baburao Patel, for example, renowned for his sarcastic tongue, wrote in the 'Howlers of the month' column of his monthly magazine *Filmindia*: 'The Wadias have released *Toofani Tarzan* at 28 stations simultaneously and threatened the entire civilisation of India. Are we going back to primitive times? Why not start a movement back-to-nature with Wadia as the first president?' Homi wasn't in the least bothered by such mean-spirited attacks on the part of intellectuals, but JBH couldn't stand being laughed at by former fellow students and sundry family members on account of his childish films. Anyone concerned with their reputation in India did not go to the cinema at all, certainly not to a stunt film. Therefore, Billimoria's suggestion struck a chord within JBH's innermost desires: the first sound picture bearing the Wadia Movietone banner he would produce was to be a 'fantasy from 1001 Nights' with Shakespearean depth. *Lal-e-Yaman* became a sumptuously produced romantic drama that, instead of the intended four weeks, ran to full houses for fourteen, making it more popular than India's first sound picture *Alam Ara*. JBH received respect not only for this achievement as a screenplay writer and director, but also for having found his way out of the dregs of stunt productions.

The financial success of *Lal-e-Yaman* encouraged the Wadia brothers to buy back their palace-like family home Lovji Castle and convert it into a studio. In the generously proportioned rooms between the oriental columns of the sweeping terrace and the balconies, beneath the roofs of lascivious green of the lush gardens, six melodramas were filmed, one after the other, in the subsequent months. While these films did not attain the rank of milestones in Indian film history, they did earn more money than they cost. This development in the direction of serious entertainment, however, brought problems of its own, blatantly revealing the differences between the brothers. JBH, the more articulate of the two, was an extensively educated intellectual who enjoyed the public appearances and the media interest of Bombay society. Homi, on the other hand, was shy and, as a doer with technical skills, preferred to withdraw to sports clubs after work. In 1934, he finally voiced his desire to JBH and Billimoria to work as a director once more and to make a film that, along the lines of the first Wadia productions, would showcase stunts and action. As a brother shouldering a paternal function, JBH felt partly responsible for Homi's career and so he rewrote the screenplay of the political drama *Veer Bharat* into a populist detective story. The cinematic cocktail of genres sold surprisingly well and the three business heads of Wadia Movietone decided on double-track production for the future. Four melodramas and two stunt films were envisaged for a year's production.

Film distribution was also part of the Wadia Movietone business, as it was for other studios at the time—apart from their own productions, studios distributed other Indian and foreign films. All said and done, JBH was still a great fan of Hollywood movies! Having made a name for himself, one of his greatest pleasures was inviting Hollywood guests visiting Bombay on a tour of the Lovji Castle Studio. Among them was the idol of JBH's youth, Douglas Fairbanks, past the zenith of his career in the USA in 1934. In India, on the other hand, his fans had never forgotten *The Thief of Baghdad* and *Zorro*, and enthusiastic receptions greeted the sporty actor wherever he cared to go. And thus it came to pass that JBH, in a mixture of admiration and business acumen, asked Douglas Fairbanks if he could show the silent movie, *The Mark of Zorro* (1920), already considered a classic, in Indian cinemas with a synchronized Hindi version and soundtrack. The deal was sealed with a handshake and JBH ensured his position as director of this experiment. When the film came to the cinemas, JBH, Homi and Billimoria went to the screenings—to the cheapest seats as before—not merely to check the audience's reactions. Their own, boyish enthusiasm for the daring, ironic action entertainment from America had been rekindled. It was precisely at this moment in the history of Wadia Movietone that Nadia made her first appearance. The timing couldn't have been better.

In the atmosphere of the rediscovered zeal for action, Nadia, in spite of the disastrous test shots, was placed on the regular salary list of Wadia Movietone.

The Newcomer in the Big Film Family

'JBH called me to his office after he had watched the test shots. "Miss Nadia," he said to me, "we would be delighted if you would stay with us. But you will have to work very, very hard! Your colleague Meherjibhai Tarapore, an extremely erudite man, will tutor you in Hindustani. You will have to spend many hours with him. I intend to cast you as an actress in a very exciting film, the screenplay to which I'm currently writing."' The success of the revival of *Zorro* had led JBH to the idea of digging out his third silent movie, also based on a Douglas Fairbanks idea. In the thriller *The Amazon*, the actress Padma was one of the first Indian women to participate in action scenes, but had to be doubled in all risky situations by stuntmen.

Since sequels were regarded as safe sources of income, and not only in India, the next film idea was in the air in 1935: a new stunt film with the title *Hunterwali*. Nadia, playing the lead role, was to perform all the risky scenes without a double. This idea, JBH later claimed, shot through his mind during his first meeting with Nadia. However, since the screenplay didn't yet exist a week after their meeting, he merely hinted at his plans to Nadia: 'Before we start with *Hunterwali*, I'd like to see how the audience reacts to you in a minor role.' Excited at the prospect, Nadia was ready to leave the office in the best of spirits when JBH called after her, informing her that he had an artiste's name for Nadia. She was to be called 'Nanda Devi' and would have to wear a black wig with long pigtails. 'A ghastly thought—I was horrified and said to him: "Look here, Mr Wadia, I am willing to try anything once, but this is ridiculous. I am a white woman and I'll look foolish with long black hair. And my name is very well known all over India as Nadia. I refuse to change my name. It has been chosen by an Armenian fortune teller and it has brought me good luck. And besides I'm no devi!" We argued about all this for a few days and luckily he saw it my way. We tested with the black wig and all but I really looked funny and so finally I remaincd myself and got to keep my stage name. And as I also told him, "Nadia even rhymes with Wadia!"'

Notwithstanding this initial defiance—uncharacteristic for a newcomer and revealing her sense of humour, a trait she shared with the Wadia brothers—Nadia withdrew to the position of the silent observer in her early days at the studio. This was also largely because she understood very little of Gujarati, which was the first language of a majority of employees. She learned her Hindustani texts that were transcribed into Latin letters and had her pronunciation corrected over and over again. In Indian sound films, Hindustani, a mixture of Hindi and Urdu, prevailed as the language understood by most people, particularly in north and central India. Within the established studio structure, the vocabulary-learning Nadia wasn't really taken seriously: in the hierarchy of those days, actors were by no means at the top of the business and would never have thought of demanding special treatment.

In this respect, Wadia Movietone—just like the other production firms in Bombay, Madras and Calcutta—functioned like a patriarchal family. Numerous employees had to appear punctually between eight and half past eight in the morning, whether or not they had work to do. And the workday ended between six and half past six. The permanent presence of the entire workforce made a very effective work routine possible, not least because the schedule of the day could be changed easily according to production requirements, depending upon the weather conditions or the granting of a long-awaited filming permit for outside locations or even availability of elephants or tigers on loan from maharajas!

Since there were no class divisions among the cameraman, the actors and the cleaning lady, only certain differences in salary, the working atmosphere at Wadia Movietone—not only in the recollection of the bosses—was extremely friendly. No one felt too superior to get on with work that wasn't directly part of their job description. If an actress wasn't in front of the camera, she would help with the hanging of curtains for the backdrop or the repairing of costumes. If the lead actor wasn't required in the final outdoor shot before lunch, he would fetch food for everyone. Even between direction and camerawork, the division of tasks was blurred.

What is referred to today as team spirit could only exist because most heads of studios looked after the crew in a manner that was almost moving. D.G. Phalke, for example, had the idea of introducing special embroidery courses for the female crew members when they had nothing to do. Himansu Rai and Devika Rani, the cosmopolitan artiste couple at the head of Bombay Talkies, had set up a school for the children of employees where tuition in acting (but naturally) was also given. The canteen at Bombay Talkies created a sensation. Here, people of all castes and every religion ate together—at a time when Brahmins elsewhere still refused, with century-old disgust, to eat food prepared by the 'untouchables'. Wadia Movietone, which provided free medical care for its employees among other benefits, enjoyed a near exemplary reputation.

The strongly developed social structures of many Indian studios were the result of a consciously political attitude of the fervent producers of those days. Back then, the film industry was considered—relatively regardless of genre—a disreputable business. Whoever decided to enter this industry from the background of a 'good family' did it from sheer enthusiasm and love for film. For the most part, this activity was even shrouded in a flair of rebellion which fitted with the progressive ideas of Mahatma Gandhi. Members of high society who got involved with cinema quite justifiably regarded themselves as pioneers. With the advent of the sound film, this self-estimation took on an additional dynamic as film-making had to be practically reinvented through this cinematic revolution. They were compelled to proceed auto-didactically, the opportunity of visiting the American or European studios for educational purposes being a rare privilege. Very few Indian production firms managed to make the leap from silent film to sound film, because of the expense alone occasioned by the equipment and the soundproofing of studios. There are a number of long-forgotten production firms described in a 'Who's Who' of Indian cinema as having had a 'short life' or as 'made one film and then bit the dust' or as 'a bright flash of lightning, disappearing just as quickly however after the first film'.

For many actors and actresses, the technical development also heralded the end of their career. Not only because their voices proved unsuitable for sound recordings—lots of performers could speak only English but none of the Indian languages, and scarcely any of the silent movie stars could sing. But in the medium term, the introduction of the microphone brought with it cinematographic and economic opportunities. 'The sound film in many ways kicked up boulders in the path of our film production firms, but from the perspective of the nationally attuned Indian, the new technology brought a lot of good with it, too.' Thus went the editor's letter of *Filmindia* on 1 April 1933. 'The preference for foreign films is gradually abating. This trend is more prevalent in west India than in Bengal and Madras. It is clear that sound films from the Western world do not really inspire the Indian fans. They are merely tolerated because of their technical superiority in camerawork and sound quality!' During the days of the silent movie, the Indian public already showed its preference for Indian stories; yet it was scarcely possible then to produce films that would bring in revenues anywhere near the costs entailed. An Indian film needed to make at least ten times as much money not to flop as compared to an American film which was doing the rounds in this secondary market.

The American studios had secured their market-leading position internationally during the First World War—the European competitors couldn't keep up either. They flooded Indian cinemas with copies of films that could be rented extremely cheaply by theatre owners. A statistical study from 1926 showed that 85 per cent of all films shown in Indian cinemas were of foreign extraction, the majority of them American. That changed when the introduction of sound film gave rise to a specifically Indian film culture. Today, on an average India produces 800 films annually, outnumbering the output in the US.

Despite the limited numbers, the 1930s witnessed studios carrying out a variety of experiments with genres, subjects, languages and length. The main criteria for a filmgoer in those days was whether you wanted to see an Imperial film, a Bombay Talkies film, a Ranjit Movietone film or a Wadia Movietone film—the names of the directors barely played a role and which studio the stars were with was common knowledge. As a consequence, many jobs—including those of props people and scenery movers—rested on whether the respective studio managed to develop a profile with their films that whetted curiosity for the next production. This 'all in the same boat' constellation called for the 'one big family' sense of belonging, the passing of which is still mourned by everyone who was there in those golden years. One example of this is an anecdote told from the time that Imperial Studios shut their gates for ever in August 1938. Around thirty employees were former criminal offenders who hadn't left the grounds for over seven years 'out of fear of the law'. They suddenly had no idea where to go and how to find their way about town any more. For days on end they camped in front of the gate in the hope that the studio with its hotel-like service would accommodate them soon again.

It is possible that in the memory of some, the wild pioneer days have been romantically idealized, for it was only by keeping the salaries extremely low that studios were able to employ several hundred permanent employees. Yet, Ismail Shaikh's account of his early years at Wadia Movietone sounds anything but bitter: 'I was about ten years old and was working at the baggage claim at the railway station. Back then the term "child labour" didn't exist, it was perfectly normal to be working at my age. I noticed a man there who had been raking around in the shelves for three days. I asked him what he was looking for. "Film canisters," he replied. Normally, no one pays heed to such things at the station but this man was searching like a madman. Eventually, I helped him look—and found the canisters. Whereupon the man asked me: "What do you earn here? You seem bright, come with me, I work in film production, you'll definitely earn more there!" The man was acquainted with Homi Wadia and he took me to him in his car. "You'll be glad to have this boy!" said the man to Homi Wadia. I had hoped the sixteen rupees I earned at the railway would rise to eighteen at the film studio. But Homi was always a sharp businessman and he said to me: "Look here, you know nothing about films, you still have a lot to learn. So to begin with you won't earn any money at all for your work." I said: "I am ten years old and have to earn money. How long would I have to learn?" Homi Wadia answered: "That depends on how fast a learner you are." In the first month I went home with nothing, in the second month I got ten rupees for travelling expenses, and just when I was about to look for a new job, Homi declared himself willing to pay me fourteen rupees.'

Ismail learned quickly and grew increasingly enthusiastic about the work. 'I had to snap the clapboard when the director shouted "action". Quick as lightning I laid it aside and crept into the picture from behind because we always had too few extras. I stayed there and acted until "cut" was shouted—and I ran to the front again and snapped the clapboard. Before the next scene, I also had to note down whether the take had been accepted or not.' Today, there are at least three people in film production firms doing what Ismail Shaikh coped with as a badly paid unskilled worker. And still he remained—and has done to this day—in his studio, 'because we always had so much fun at work'.

Slave for the Masses

It was in this experimental phase of the early days of the sound film that Nadia arrived at Wadia Movietone. The film technicians were scratching their heads about how best to imbue the action-packed stunt films with sound. Or should the studio rather concentrate on the production of other films? J.B.H. Wadia favoured the latter which corresponded more closely to his intellectual inclinations. He had also achieved considerable success as director in the field of melodrama, a genre taken seriously by critics as well. And thus it was decided that Nadia's screen presence should be tested in one of the more high-brow light entertainment films before she take up the lead in *Hunterwali*. The film *Desh Deepak* was already in production and Nadia got a minor role. Filmed on fire-endangered nitrate film, only a few hand-coloured metres have survived. Fortunately, among them is the song sequence that became a real hit: *Dil pher mera zalim/ Hans hans key churaneywale* ... (*Make my heart whirl, my heartless beloved/Your smile has stolen my heart* ...)

In another scene, considered one of the treasures of the film archive in Pune, Nadia plays a slave up for auction. She writhes on a dais in front of an imaginary audience. To the left of her feet, a small, moustachioed merchant praises her qualities. First you see Nadia half turned away from the audience, her arms clutching her chest. Then she turns around—and from the shy slave-girl rises a proud woman who is perfectly aware of the effect she is having. She sways her hips elegantly in her golden skirt, stretches her arms to the side so that her scantily clad bosom is seen to maximum effect. In the subsequent close-ups, two unforgettable blue eyes flash, then a cherry-red mouth smiles, and in the third close-up we see her perfect pearl-white teeth. There are 'ohs' and 'ahs' from the invisible public and a new star is discovered. That scene, to a certain extent a fictionally exaggerated replay of her interview with J.B.H. Wadia, had the first fan mail trickling in for 'the blonde' at Wadia Movietone. Yet, her Hindustani was still too poor for the lead role in *Hunterwali* and Nadia was tested for a second time in a minor role.

In *Noor-e-Yaman*, a musical melodrama, Nadia had a few lines as one of the two sisters of the hero. Among them: '*Jab dil na raha kabu mein toh meri khata kya*.' Since she had no idea that this sentence dealt with a heart racing out of control, she said 'Kabul'—a city she had the most pleasant memories of—instead of 'kabu', each and every time. Again and again the scene had to be repeated. Nadia was about to be thrown out as her inability to speak the lines threatened to ruin the whole film in spite of the smallness of her role. Equally fraught was the filming of an extremely sentimental scene. 'I was playing the role of Princess Parizad. The child star Firoze Dastur was supposed to die in that scene. JBH came to me and commanded, "Weep now!" I looked at him: "Weep?" "Yes, yes, yes! Go on, weep! I want you to weep!" I couldn't help myself—when I heard him talking like this I got a laughing fit. How was I to weep now? "Get a move on and weep," he shouted, spitting with rage. I couldn't control myself. The others started raging too—only the extras found the situation funny and started to giggle with me. Finally, I was laughing so hard that tears came. JBH yelled: "Quickly! She has tears in her eyes—a close-up now, quickly!" I'll never forget that moment—it was hilarious!'

The First Leap from the Roof

In December 1934, preparations for the production of the next extravagant melodrama from Wadia Movietone shuddered to a halt because the lead actress fell ill. The screenplay for the planned stunt film with Nadia in the lead role had been completed in the meantime. The story of *Hunterwali* (roughly *Lady with the Whip* in English) was tailor-made for Nadia. JBH pushed for this rather small and cheap production to be given priority so as not to waste too much studio time. Homi Wadia was sceptical for he doubted the talents of the blonde lead.

'Homi didn't know how to approach the job,' Minoo Tampal, the sound engineer, recalls. 'Miss Nadia was a white lady after all and everyone in the studio felt out of their element when asked to work with her as a stunt actress. Back then she was still very reserved, very quiet, and a far cry from messing around like a buddy with those of us who had been on the team longer. I think it had to do with her not speaking Gujarati. At the same time, she was very professional and came to work every morning just like us. In those days the studio functioned almost like a factory, there were even time-cards that we had stamped each morning. Afterwards we were told what had to be done in the course of the day, depending on which film we were currently working on. Homi Wadia told us which scenes were planned; the screenplays came from J.B.H. Wadia. These instructions were taken as seriously as the Bible and carried out meticulously by everyone. But I still remember how our routine was somehow thrown into confusion during the first production discussion of *Hunterwali*. The screenplay envisaged a great number of stunts and fight scenes for Nadia, although there were also palace scenes in which she—traditionally feminine—was to appear in a sari and had some dialogues to deliver. That's where we wanted to start, with these simple tasks. Unfortunately, the set designer said that wouldn't be possible because the intricate scenery wasn't complete when filming began. We pondered back and forth until Homi Wadia decided that we should begin with the fight scene on the roof. Nadia had to fight some bodyguards at quite a height and then leap from the roof. It was a very tricky stunt scene that would have been a real challenge even for our experienced stuntmen like Boman Shroff and Ustad Haque. We didn't believe Nadia capable of it. In the studio the news spread like wildfire that our director planned to start with that of all scenes ... but no one dared suggest something easier to him. Meanwhile, Nadia turned to Homi Wadia and said: "I've heard I am to jump from a roof? Which one is it then?" Upon which he went outside with Nadia and showed her the sharp steep roof, about five metres high. She looked at it and simply said: "Okay." We were fairly amazed—and feared the worst.'

Not long before, an experienced Wadia stuntman had almost drowned, having miscalculated a jump from a freight ship. In general, scrapes, dislocated joints and often more severe injuries were part of the daily fare. Nadia may have practised some jumps and falls under the guidance of experienced stunt people on the studio training area—however, most members in the team had an uneasy feeling when the coconut was smashed on the first day of filming. This so-called mahurat ritual, customary in all Indian studios, is supposed to bring good fortune to the film and protect the film-makers from misfortune and mishaps.

'Nadia was the only one who was confident and in good spirits that day. We made the final preparations, set up the camera, the other stunt people were dressed in police uniforms. They climbed onto the roof—and the first take was flawless. Nadia was masked and made a convincing bandit. One after the other, left and right she punched them from the roof and paid not the slightest heed to the camera. But then came the dreaded wide shot where she was supposed to jump down. Apparently, Homi Wadia was rather nervous too, as he sent for Mr Dhunbhoora, regarded by everyone as an experienced "bone-setter". Scarcely was he on hand than Nadia was back on the roof again—and Homi called "action". Nadia hesitated, but only for the fraction of a second, and leapt. Everyone held their breath. Her landing was perfect! Today it's impossible to imagine what working conditions were like then—Nadia had nothing more than a thin mattress to land on. When the cameraman said "okay", Homi shouted "cut". But Nadia didn't get up—so we all ran over and looked at her with worried expressions to see what was wrong. Nadia looked at us with suffering in her eyes, until she could no longer suppress her laughter. That was the moment I will never forget—her wonderful laughter, our bafflement that ended in enthusiastic spontaneous applause. After work that day, we were called into the office and Homi Wadia gave a little speech. He said that the first day of filming was the prelude to a most special film and we should all work together better than ever. Then he congratulated Nadia on her courage and called her "fearless". From that day forth she was "Fearless Nadia".'

Cover of programme booklet for Hunterwali

The Princess Becomes the Stunt Queen

J.B.H. Wadia's idea of making a stunt queen of a woman sprung from his old admiration for American serial heroines such as Pearl White, Helen Holmes, Ruth Holland, Grace

Cunard and Marie Walcamp. However, for the story of *Hunterwali*, he had drawn inspiration from Douglas Fairbanks's *Robin Hood*, the great-grandfather of all cloak-and-dagger films. He combined both these recipes for success and transferred them to an imaginary mystical Indian kingdom, and something unconventionally new came into being.

This Wadia Movietone kingdom, a good seventy years after its creation, seems touchingly naïve at first. From the coarsely constructed palace setting it is clear that only people from a poor background could take the somewhat ridiculous fountain, gates and halls to be the home of a royal family.

Nadia is Madhuri, the daughter of an ageing king who is threatened by the putsch attempts of the evil minister Ranamal (played by Sayani 'Atish'). One day, when Nadia is returning to the palace after an excursion, Ranamal causes a bad car accident: Jaswant (Boman Shroff), a man begging for milk, is dragged under the wheels. Nadia rushes over to him, but is held back: 'You mustn't touch him!' Nadia nonetheless insists on driving the injured man to hospital. Later, the good king has the beggar brought to him and offers him money as compensation for the pains suffered. He refuses. This proud gesture pleases Nadia as much as it does her father and there's a feeling that a romance may be budding.

A little later, Nadia is sitting at the piano, well-groomed in a sari, when the devious Ranamal tells her that her father has been kidnapped, and could possibly have been killed. This has brought him one step closer to his goal—succession to the throne. Now he has to marry the princess. However, the clever daughter of the king already senses that Ranamal himself is the kidnapper. Barely has the father been kidnapped than the action begins. To today's audience, the action may seem funny rather than exciting—but it is still rousing. A great rumpus follows during which Nadia is initiated into politics. For the first time in her life the rich princess discovers just how far the evil minister has already pushed the regime of injustice—the kidnapping of her old, weak father is only one piece in the jigsaw puzzle of his diabolical endeavours.

Surrounded by plaintive friends from the so-called simple folk, Nadia stands gravely in the midst of the gathering, and her gaze sweeps to the whip on the wall. With an expression of resolve she grabs it, cracks it and solemnly swears that revenge shall be hers from now on. All those present seal the vow by placing their hands on Hunterwali's new symbol by which she will be henceforth recognized. Yet, she is still clad—femininity personified—in a dark sari!

In a skilled piece of drama, a few alcohol-drenched swaggering statements by men serve as a prelude to her first appearance as 'avenger of those stripped of their rights'. In a dive, cowardly, bragging soldiers are laughing at Hunterwali as though she were a ghost that hard men don't believe in. Seemingly out of thin air, she is suddenly on the small balcony above the doorway, cracking her whip and sending, by way of a greeting, a barrel of whisky flying into the circle of men with all her might, laughing provocatively. 'I have come to show you who I really am!' Even a less wild entrance would have had the audience of the 1930s gasping for breath: the transformed king's daughter had traded her chaste sari for extremely daring shorts revealing two spectacularly muscular thighs. Moreover, she now sported erotically tight-fitting, knee-length boots, and a scanty, sleeveless blouse with an elegantly jaunty cape fluttering about it. The magnificent head of blonde hair is tucked beneath a Russian-like fur cap. The black eye-mask completes the disguise to perfection. Thus adorned, Fearless Nadia leaps into the male domain, provocation made flesh, and—laughing contemptuously—starts thrashing up to ten men at a time! Nadia determines the dynamics of the fighting, she dishes out punches, cracks her whip wildly, rushes up the stairs and down in the thick of it. The fighting, far from feeble, comes over so playfully, as though nothing could be more fun for this strong woman than knocking the living daylights out of this flock of idiotic machos. No sooner are the weaklings defeated than Nadia is pole-vaulting to the archway—and in the next scene she disappears into the palace again through a secret passage. Quick as a flash she is back to being a crimped princess ready to confront her most dangerous rival who questions her on the dangerous Hunterwali. 'Why don't you just go to her?' Nadia asks cheekily—at which point he proposes marriage to her, for the third time. In response he gets nothing but loud peals of laughter. The absurd notion of marrying such a person sends the princess into painful paroxysms of laughter.

Constantly moving back and forth between her staid palace life and her adventurous existence as a fighting, climbing, riding, courageous 'Lady Robin Hood', Nadia—the Good—triumphs, as is obligatory in Indian cinema, over Evil. First, though, a reward of 1000 rupees is placed on her head and she has to traverse numerous tests and trials to get the better of the unjust regime. Time and again she leaps unexpectedly to the side of her loyal followers just at the moment they need help: where someone is being unfairly whipped, she knocks the whip from the tormentor's grasp. She crouches like a tigress in the trees and, should the situation require it, swings on vines onto the back of the galloping horse of her enemy. In the course of the story, the rather handsome beggar, Jaswant, becomes her companion, and also chances upon her at the river where Nadia refreshes herself from her many scraps, wearing nothing more than a bra and a little slip. At the end, not only is the old father freed, but a rape is avenged, too, and, thanks to a very unconventional woman, happy harmony restored for all concerned. It's left to the viewer's imagination whether the old king is reinstated or whether the good-looking comrade-in-arms at Nadia's side becomes heir to his potential father-in-law. It is of course also conceivable that Nadia as a single heroine takes on this lofty position.

During filming, Homi Wadia, stimulated by the abilities of his new star, grew more and more daring. In the production office it had long since been agreed that the internal studio name 'Fearless Nadia' would also be built into the publicity strategy. To live up to this image, Homi Wadia came up daily with new ideas of things Nadia could do. Simply imitating everything that only men had done formerly wasn't enough for him. One day—Nadia was back up on a roof—Homi called: 'Lift him up—and carry him around!' 'Never in my life had I carried a man, but as I say, I'll try anything once. And so I heaved my stunt partner onto my shoulders. Homi liked it—and ever since he's been commanding me to drag all manner of men around the place.'

A little later, filming was unexpectedly interrupted. After a tiring day which Nadia had spent entirely on horseback, one scene had to be redone in the studio. Nadia was supposed to swing through a room, from a stair-landing onto a chandelier, to escape from her enemies. It was a risky scene, and J.B.H. Wadia suggested using a double for Nadia for the stunt. At the rehearsal, someone was standing by to catch her in case of an emergency—but everything ran smoothly. During the shooting, however, the rope snapped and Nadia fell from quite a height, landing awkwardly on the floor. 'For three days I couldn't move. I lay at home and the whole time my mother kept at me, trying to persuade me: "If you keep going with this madness you're asking for your death"—oh, well, just what mothers say in such situations.' For several weeks, Nadia was helplessly at the mercy of her mother's tirade. But she didn't cave in and went back to the studio as soon as the doctor allowed.

In the meantime, the Wadia brothers, having watched the finished material several times, were sure they had a hit on their hands. JBH pumped more money into the film than originally envisaged to insert some additional songs and romantic scenes which he directed himself. Only their business partner Billimoria got cold feet—he was afraid that the Wadia brothers had let their enthusiasm for Miss Nadia turn their heads. To his mind the film had become too radical. As often before, his business sense hadn't deceived him. When *Hunterwali* was finally finished, six months later, they couldn't find any cinema owner willing to take on the risk. A blonde heroine who fought Indian men and, to top it off, is anything but modestly attired? Lots of men who had previously been regarded as dependable business partners in the marketing of Wadia films, considered *Hunterwali* too bold, too risky—and jumped ship.

Finally, JBH, Homi and Billimoria decided to take the film to the cinema on their own steam with a lavish advertising budget. In Super Cinema on Grant Road a film had been cancelled and the cinema manager was looking for a replacement. That seemed the right place for the *Hunterwali* premiere! A cinema programme was also printed: '*Hunterwali*! What visions does that film stir up! It is the story of a brave Indian girl who sacrificed royal luxury to the cause of her people and country.' The advertisements in the film magazines showed the drawing of a woman: Nadia sitting on a rearing horse, whip in her hand. Beneath it the slogan: 'A spectacular thriller, the first of its kind in India!'

'From This Day Forth Call Me "Hunterwali!"'

On the evening of the premiere, the screening was sold out and more. Nadia arrived with her mother and Bobby. 'I was so nervous that my whole body was trembling. I spent the whole time looking around and trying to gauge the reactions on the faces of the audience. Mummy had to hold my left hand, Bobby my right. My first appearance was in the second reel, fifteen minutes into the film, and when my voice was heard I heard the public gasping for breath. They were stunned by my performance. In the third reel I swear I'll avenge my father's abduction and free him from the clutches of the evil minister. Then I crack the whip and say: "From this day forth call me Hunterwali!" At that point the audience went wild. They just didn't stop whistling and applauding!'

In cinema-loving Bombay, the news spread overnight: a new face had made it into the galaxy of stars, an actress like there had never been before! Nadia didn't only look completely different to the dark-haired, meek beauties, her behaviour on-screen was also in complete contrast to the submissive, weak, dependent-on-men ladies of the screen. Once again it was proven that the distributors and cinema managers, the most conservative branch in the film business, had nervously underestimated the hunger of the public for a new, surprising, and never-before-seen phenomenon.

Hunterwali rapidly became the most successful film of the season and was shown all over the country for more than twenty-five weeks. And Wadia Movietone no longer had to bother with advertising. *Hunterwali* fever gripped the whole of India. In every market and bazaar there were whips, masks and miniature 'Hunterwali' pictures on sale. The film became a huge success and outstripped the wildest hopes of its makers. Through *Hunterwali*, Wadia Movietone had gained a clear profile. The experimental phase of the early sound film days were over for the time being. Nadia's monthly wage was most generously increased—while many of her acting colleagues of the traditional school were dismissed with a few kind words. It was clear to the Wadia brothers that they had to build a new ensemble around the new star. And thus began a fevered search for bodybuilders with acting talent and trained animal stars.

3
3

HER OWN ROLE MODEL

HER OWN ROLE MODEL

Lutaru Lalna, 1938

After a relatively short 'apprenticeship', by 1935, Fearless Nadia had become one of the biggest stars in the Indian film business: famous, admired and yet a world away from ascending the respected circles of the late colonial society. This was the fate Nadia shared with the majority of her colleagues. Any woman who even dared approach a film studio, risked her good name.

'Are the fans justified in the following remark: "The other name for an educated 'prostitute' is the 'film actress'?"' This is the question, for example, posed by an anonymous writer from Jammu in the readers' page of *Filmindia* in October 1937. The editor, Baburao Patel, known for his acerbic tongue, replied to the question he had in all probability formulated himself: 'They are not only not justified in saying so but they are erring rather sadly. Every film actress is more or less a devotee at the Altar of Art. To call them prostitutes is to invite a question on the sanity of the person who thinks so. I have met the best of them, and I doubt if any of them can merit the low epithet. Someday I shall give you the definition of the word prostitute and tell you what a glorious part a prostitute plays in the life of a nation. She is more an object of pity than of scorn.'

Baburao Patel was one of the central figures of the eccentric Bombay film scene in the 1930s and 1940s. His magazine *Filmindia* was both the feared central organ and fiercely loved Bible of the scene, but equally a gossip rag read by fans and those with an interest in cinema, containing all important insider information. Among this was the latest from the studios, film reviews, political debates about war propaganda and questions of censorship. *Filmindia* was published in English and was primarily conceived for a well-heeled, educated readership that was indeed interested in cinema but at the same time took seriously the reservations about this business regarded as disreputable. This discourse even today almost exclusively focuses on actresses. In India, female professionals in the film business have to meet extremely delicate expectations. Regardless of individual conduct, of appearance and of the roles played, the guardians of morality keep raising the question whether for a woman it is not indecent per se to be put on display in front of so many men, even if the actress on the screen, according to the common code of tradition, is acting in the most chaste of saris and with exemplary femininity. This is the favourite dilemma of the film industry as intellectuals consider the many dimensions of its problematic nature with relish and a certain smugness.

A college student in June 1941 described the difficulties an Indian man faced when looking for an ideal woman amongst the current top stars. He said very frankly in advance that this actress would have to be the right one to dream of day or night and be able, at least in a platonic manner, to satisfy the demands of his suppressed sexuality. Then he ran through all the current beauties, assessing them: the first one was too old for him, the second he couldn't see yet in suitable roles so she remained unapproachable to him 'like a flower without fragrance'. With the third he was afraid of rejection, the fourth seemed too shy, the fifth had too childlike a form for his liking and he couldn't wait forever. The sixth seemed too individualist, the seventh too serious, with the eighth her Bengali accent was irritating, when she was silent, though, he considered her virtually ideal. Finally, the sole remaining lady was the enchanting Leela Chitnis whom his friends enthused about too, and all girls who wanted to be noticed by him in real life had to bring to mind, when they blushed, at least a touch of Leela Chitnis. But then *Filmindia*, in June 1941, published an article on this object of worship, describing her as the 'champion mother' amongst the stars. 'And with these words the famous critic shatters our dream and writes the saddest epitaph on our romance. A mother! Can a champion mother be a heroine to the dreamy youth? And who wants a mother for our heroine—certainly not the college boys. The place in our heart therefore goes vacant crying for a candidate.'

The candid blurring between the big screen and the real world must have been very widespread—such is the seduction of cinema in whatever cultural circle. Magazines like *Filmindia* live from this phenomenon and articles designed like detailed marriage announcements are often to be found there about female stars. An example is the portrait of Leela Desai in 1942. In it, one didn't merely discover that she lived all alone in Bombay's chic millionaires' quarter and that at home she preferred to dress simply and wore hardly any make-up, but also how she envisaged her dream man. On no account did Leela Desai want to marry an actor. She was repelled by arrogant, rich men and was looking for a manly, generous-hearted and hard-working 'Mr Right'. As soon as he was found from amongst her numerous fans she would stop acting, for she was convinced that there can be no happiness in a household where both husband and wife work. With this confession and its underlying message of obedience, Leela Desai was over the first barrier: as an unmarried actress she may be adored and courted by countless wooers but she pledged to give up this status of her own free will as soon as she belonged completely to the chosen one.

Now, as then, in India this classic whore–housewife double bind is resolved upon entering into marriage which brings a more or less automatic end to a female acting career, exceptions proving the rule. Incidentally, this was also true of Indian stewardesses for a long time. How self-evidently the interests of the professional woman are ignored can be seen in a reader's letter to *Filmindia* asking whether women who have worked as actresses are contemptuous of marriage. On the contrary, says Baburao Patel, all actresses were keen to marry, because for them, as for every other woman, the harbour of marriage alone offers the prospect of a tranquil, contented future. And it wasn't only from a male perspective that it appeared self-evident and normal that producers and cinema fans would lose interest in an actress once it was known she was embarking upon marriage. Consequently, a female columnist in *Filmindia* wrote about the 'right' of fans to know something about the private life of a famous film star! And thus, on the readers' letters pages, questions regarding weight, height, age, salary, caste and addresses of individual actresses were answered regularly—in the style characteristic of contact advertisements.

Although one of the top female stars in the 1930s and 1940s, Fearless Nadia was assigned an interesting, exotic position in this cinema-oriented marriage market. All through her long career she remained single, but from her first film *Hunterwali*, she escaped being straitjacketed in the rigid role models for female characters on-screen and created a new one for herself. Her unmarried status fitted with her sacrosanct autonomy since on the screen she either never married or simply doubled up with laughter when suggestions of this nature were made. Nonetheless, an anonymous, curious C.R.R. from Nellore wanted to know: 'Who is Nadia? Why do the Wadia brothers take her up for every picture they produce? Can't they get any other good and charming girl?' Thc editor who probably himself formulated this question, responded mysteriously: 'Nadia is a foreign girl. People suspect her of having come from some circus. As long as the Wadias think that Nadia is beautiful, it does not matter to us. I personally think that in all the jungle pictures that Wadia has produced, Nadia is a suitable heroine. A more charming girl, as you require, simply would not fit in with the jungle.'

Nadia encountered less mercy in the article of a reporter by the name of Hyacinth in *Filmindia* in April 1942. She described how men, through Hollywood cinema, had become more 'aware of legs' and as a consequence want to 'see facts' from Indian actresses as well. This poses endless problems for these ladies, according to Hyacinth, for 'God' has 'blessed' them with a stature shown to advantage only in a sari. For good or for bad, following the dictates of fashion, the Indian filmgoer caught more and more glimpses of 'fleshy hips'. Yet the sight of what came tumbling out of the swimming costume of one of the adored was enough to cause even an uncritical fan to fall out of love. 'A few of the braver, or should we say less sensitive souls among our actresses, have ventured before the cameras in shorts, and now our Fearless Nadia is wearing a good imitation of a Dorothy Lamourish sarong. We make no criticism of her but we would just like to emphasise the fact that we think she is very fearless indeed to let the public see her like that!' In an even meaner tone, Nadia is taunted in a reader's letter from a certain Krishna Murthy for her 'un-American' build. Referring to her admirable riding skills apparent in the cinema, he wanted to know why Nadia hadn't actually become a jockey as she surely could have made lots of money on the racetrack. The answer goes: 'And what about the poor horse? It would have been a case for the cruelty to animals brigade!'

Of course all these scathing commentaries on her person can be read differently: Nadia, who fights like a man on-screen and is often more scantily attired than most of her colleagues, doesn't, quite simply, play the game. Neither in *Hunterwali* nor in her numerous later roles does she epitomize the dream-lady type, the sort that every male viewer immediately wants to fetch from the cinema to their stove at home. Also, she obviously doesn't care to conform to the ideal of beauty imported from the USA that dictates an actress should have legs like Marlene Dietrich. She shows her muscular thighs and her ample physique in a self-confident manner, as though she is very much aware that in India a different, older standard of beauty exists. In 1978, a film reporter, recollecting Nadia and some popular acting colleagues, wrote in the magazine *Picture Post*: 'The skinny actresses were always at a disadvantage compared to the large ones from a historical perspective ... regardless of which of our old frescoes or paintings is taken as a reference, my point will be substantiated. The temple of Konark alone is proof enough of my contention that Indian people have always been enchanted by voluptuous, strapping women.'

Nadia had outsmarted the anti-feminist screen alternative of housewife or whore in an elegant manner. No one accused her of wanting to use her acting to only land a good catch in real life. And from this position she was able to glide, with considerable grace, over the thin ice of the allegation of easy virtue hurled at women in the profession.

The First Heroine Had a Moustache

Nadia's producer J.B.H. Wadia had a difficult time, from his earliest boyhood, coming to terms with the morality of Indian films—in particular the depiction of female characters. That he was a Parsi probably made it all the more difficult. The Parsis are a minuscule religious minority in India that differ from the Hindu majority or the larger Muslim minority through their progressive outlook of women. Thus, JBH looked on at the portrayal of women in Indian cinema as an outsider; he felt that the female roles were consistently given too submissive a leaning. Actresses devotedly obeyed and did all that the film-husbands or film-fathers commanded. And if the film-husband enjoyed the pleasures of a film-prostitute, the film-wife naturally kept her mouth shut and didn't stop her godlike spouse. Such behaviour was just as incomprehensible and suspicious to JBH in cinema as in real life. As a producer and screenwriter in the entertainment sector, he decided to champion the emancipation of women in India. In Nadia he had found the appropriate actress. She went beyond the scope of what had gone before, and on the big screen she personified a break from tradition.

In the distant past, long before the birth of Christ, so the story goes in the history of Indian theatre, there was an early heyday of the arts of dancing, music and art. According to Hindu belief, the god Brahma, the creator of the universe, also wrote the *Natyaveda*, the holy book of dramaturgy. The *Natyaveda* teaches that every drama should be created from the four elements of language, song, dance and acting. With the aim of encouraging, entertaining, spreading happiness and advising, every performance should represent a multitude of emotional states in the most varied of situations and, in accordance with Hindu philosophy, end with the hero's victory. In around 1000 BC or thereabouts, there arose such an abundance of plays adhering to these specifications that this era came to be known as the 'Golden Age'. In those days, according to historiography, man and woman coexisted in a manner—and not just on the stage—as would be called emancipated today. The rights of Indian women were, however, severely reduced shortly before the turn of the millennium—a fact for which historians hold the Aryans responsible. These people who immigrated to the subcontinent from Central Europe gradually established the caste system to prevent the mixing of their own tribe with other ethnic groups. The result was an exclusive limitation of the freedom of movement, above all for women in the higher strata of society: apparently only total control over the fair sex could offer the men the desired security. It is still disputed whether the wretched tradition of placing many women in complete 'purdah'—the Indian equivalent of the harem—was established in the first fifteen centuries, as also the practice of locking them away and sometimes marrying them while still children. Some historians claim that this extreme form of depriving women of their rights only came with the conquering of the vast Indian subcontinent by the Muslim Mughal rulers from the north in the sixteenth century. The past 2000 years have brought scarcely any new rights to women, particularly during the British colonial time when Victorian etiquette and prudishness strengthened the discriminatory tendency all the more. For theatre and the art of Indian dance, the disappearance of women from public life led to men playing the female roles. An exception existed in the case of temple dancers and prostitutes in the art of dancing.

The connections between theatre, dance, music and prostitution remained so closely entwined well into the twentieth century that any official attempt to limit prostitution simultaneously represented a threat to the dramatic arts. The consequences for cinema were first felt by the father of Indian cinema, D.G. Phalke. He knew that filming made different demands on the realism of scenes than the stage did and therefore he wanted a woman to play the female lead in his first film *Raja Harishchandra*. It was 1912 when he went looking around the red-light district of Bombay for a suitable performer. Although the impoverished director offered the few interested parties more money than they would normally earn, all the prostitutes turned the film work down—it was beneath their dignity! Eventually, Phalke discovered an effeminate waiter by the name of A. Salunke in a restaurant. After a long period of persuasion, the young man agreed—again only on condition that he would earn considerably more than in his present job. Nonetheless, this casting almost failed because Salunke had a moustache and was extremely reluctant to shave it off. Phalke succeeded in convincing Salunke of the necessary shave, and so it came to pass that the first heroine in the annals of Indian film was a man.

Daughters from Good Families Discover the Movies

No history of Indian film omits the Salunke anecdote because it marks the beginning of a tradition that has repercussions on the reputation of the business to the present day. It is true that Indian film pioneers in this early phase almost exclusively worked with prostitutes who made acting a side job. Yet, with every passing year, the silent movies from Europe and the USA swept in an irrevocable erosion of the strict moral rules, particularly in liberal Western-oriented city circles. Most young Anglo-Indian and Jewish women were guided by other standards than their Hindu and Muslim contemporaries. It was natural that many of them had a school and further education, and the young ladies—with movie actresses from the West as their models—strove to be up-to-date fashionably and socially. From these urban circles, Indian directors and producers were soon able to recruit their female stars. To lend the ladies with their Western airs something genuinely Indian from the word go, they were generally bequeathed fine-sounding names. One of the first Anglo-Indian actresses was Marian Hill alias Vilochana. The exceedingly popular Sulochana was known in civilian life as Ruby Meyers and was of Jewish origin as were the 'Peach Sisters', Sophia and Esther Abraham, alias Romila and Pramila. Renée Smith made her career as Sita Devi and so on. With the emergence of the beautiful Durga Khote came a decisive point in the history of Indian movie actresses, the importance of which cannot be emphasized enough. Though born into a Brahmin household, she took to films. In a delicious twist of irony, in *Ayodhyecha Raja/ Ayodhya Ka Raja* (an early sound feature directed by V. Shantaram) she played the same role that the waiter A. Salunke had played in D.G. Phalke's *Raja Harishchandra*! Indirectly, this sensational discovery of an actress was thanks to J.B.H. Wadia: while he was still working in the laboratory of the Kohinoor Studios, the producer Mohan Bhavani had turned to the young man one day with the request of finding an educated lady from well-to-do society to act. With his excellent connections in those circles, JBH seemed the right man for the job. He turned to a student friend, the unanimous star in his university class. She declined without a moment's thought but recommended her sister. And this sister was Durga Khote.

However, a respected family background on its own wasn't sufficient to shield young actresses from the suspicion that they would sink in the squalor and corruption of the studio. One of Nadia's early rivals in that star-studded galaxy was Beryl Doyley, alias Madhuri, born in 1917. She grew up as the carefully sheltered daughter of Bombay's Secretary of State, a Dutchman who was married to an Anglo-Indian woman. Her father, the eighty-one-year-old Madhuri recalls, was horrified to hear that a friend of the family considered his daughter photogenic and wanted to introduce her to the movies. With the help of her mother, however, the then fourteen-year-old managed to persuade her father to let her play her first female lead role. On one condition: whenever she set foot in a film studio, her elder brother was to be at her side. Similar arrangements with chaperones, also mothers or sisters depending on the family constellation, were quite usual.

Madhuri relates how she herself accepted the film offer with enthusiasm: 'Just like Nadia I loved ballet as a girl, liked going to the cinema and dreamed of leading a life like the cover girls of *Cosmopolitan.* In my gypsy skirt with a big silk shawl around my shoulders, I performed a few steps and turned a few pirouettes, which went down well with the audience. Later, I was known as the "Sweetheart of the North" because I was particularly popular in north India—in contrast to Nadia who had fans all over the country, but different ones to mine. Nadia and I didn't know each other personally in those days, but there was a professional jealousy between us. In the thirties I was considered one of the ten top actresses and my position was shaky just when Nadia was surging upwards.'

Who was considered the best was not a question of the taste of film critics or for that matter anyone else: it was a question of money and viewer quotas. The monthly salary of the top actors was set according to the success or failure of individual productions, and not only was this sum public knowledge, but also a kind of trademark and a ubiquitously accepted measure of talent and fame. Madhuri, for example, seventy years on, still remembers exactly that her starting salary was 750 rupees a month, while the silent-movie star Sulochana with her 5000 rupees was temporarily earning more than the mayor of Bombay. Nadia with her monthly 4000 rupees was also in the upper echelons: she was the gold mine of her studio.

These sums were so fabulously high that they called plenty of envious voices into the arena. Their spokesperson was once again *Filmindia* editor Baburao Patel in December 1937. Using the example of the eight best-earning actresses, he calculated that seen in the light of production costs involved, not one of the ladies was truly worth her fee: 'The so-called stars themselves did not show any improvement in their work and were quite satisfied with ambitious increments in salaries from month to month at the sacrifice of honesty to their own act.' Patel thus skilfully turns the tables. He interprets the nerve-racking competitive struggle amongst the top stars as the women's dubious greed. Perhaps it is not surprising that many of the divas of the day remember the exact figures of fees, not only their own, while forgetting the title of one or other of their films. This may also have to do with the fact that money must have been the impetus for the majority of actresses at the time to enter the business in the first place. Though this logic is understandable, the continual harping on the subject and size of fees strikes an unconscious echo with the old connection between actresses and woman up for sale.

Filmindia regarded the increasing presence of film actresses from better society as a welcome opportunity to reflect afresh upon the popular theme of cinema and prostitution. 'We refuse to believe that it is impossible to abjure sex entanglements in motion pictures occasionally to cater to the taste of rapidly growing picture critics ...' the Bengali magazine *Filmland* wrote in July 1933. Through numerous articles in the hundreds of film magazines in India, the readership discovered how, with the educated ladies in the spotlight, the 'standard' of the industry was improving by the month. With lamentations about wayward daughters from good families and fireside tales about reformed ex-prostitutes sacrificing themselves as actresses to the point of suicide for the comfort of their husbands, these magazines examined the topic exhaustively, critically and from every imaginable angle. At the same time, those looking down at the people involved in the film business from an overly pious, moralizing stance were dealt strict warnings and scolding.

Baburao Patel was prudent enough to bring countless Indian films into the debate. Sporting the title 'Pimps and Prostitutes: Why do film stars allow themselves to be slandered, by the public, the gutter press—and by their own films?' an article appeared in May 1940. It started by ruminating at length on the hypocritical reasons for treating actresses with contempt, then went on to criticize cinema itself as the driving force behind the malicious campaigns: 'The most preposterous thing, however, is that the film stars are being constantly slandered by their own films. Take any Indian film in which one of the characters is a film star—it is the same story from *Cinema Girl* to *Laxmi*—and you would know what I mean. In these pictures, the film star is depicted as a woman of loose morals and the studio atmosphere is shown as being far from healthy. The worst offender, it is regrettable to observe, was the recent Huns' picture *In Search of Happiness* in which the character of Chanchala provided a most cruel caricature of a film star. The studio life depicted in New Theatre's *Millionaire* was not very inspiring. In *Maen Hari*, Ragini, the film star, looks at the bare body of a young fisherman and falls in love with him and brings him to town, living with him apparently on terms of intimacy without marriage. What kind of impression can the public take home from such pictures? They say to themselves: "Well, these producers ought to know how the film stars behave. Perhaps they are even worse than they are depicted in these films." And thus the slander is spread, and the irony is that the stars themselves help to spread it. The producers, perhaps, like to keep up this false impression in the public mind for reasons of their own.'

Good Sister, Bad Sister

Using the example of the film in films, Patel describes the almost schizophrenic situation for actresses, valid far beyond this particular cinematic case. Commercially successful cinema in India is actually familiar with only two exaggerated women types: the good, submissive mother/wife/sister/daughter suffering in silence with scarcely a life to call her own, existing solely for the father/husband/brother/son. Her depraved counterpart is recognizable immediately in Indian cinema by the vulgar

Western manners she cultivates. Often dressed in trousers or other European attire, she smokes, drinks, associates with men, and, as a rule, dies at the end of the film. It's also true for Nadia that with the success of *Hunterwali*, her type was established—but hers is a special case in Indian film history. In *Muqabala*, this situation is picked out as a central theme in a self-referential manner. This Wadia Movietone thriller stars Nadia in a double role. It was the first film not directed by Homi Wadia, but by debutants Nanabhai Bhatt, who also wrote the screenplay, and Babubhai Mistri, freshly poached from Prakash Studios.

Muqabala, 1942

The film *Muqabala* takes place in Himatpur and the beautiful region fits well with the happy family and the home of the two delightful twins Rani and Madhuri. One fateful day, a dangerous-looking man dressed in a coat and hat turns up and threatens the idyll with his revolver.

As the viewer discovers, he is here to exact his revenge on the mother of the twin girls whom he had wanted to marry! And bang—she's dead. The father barely escapes with his life. As the sisters are witness to the crime, the murderer seizes the little girls. Madhuri manages, however, to break free from his powerful grasp. While her sister Rani is abducted by the villain, Madhuri, in her panicked flight, runs right beneath the tyres of the only car visible for miles around. The driver decides at the site of the accident to adopt the victim of misfortune.

The film proper begins after the prologue—'20 years later'. Cruel fate cast the girls into situations which couldn't resemble one another less. Nadia–Madhuri grows up in a rich, liberal family. In the opening scene, the good-natured father tries to encourage his daughter to embark upon some housework, but is only amused when Nadia opts to go jogging instead in her tight-fitting striped blouse. She runs merrily and inquisitively through the neighbourhood, further and further on, until she comes across a strange estate. She hears odd noises coming from within. She enters the building, full of curiosity, and discovers a man lying on the ground, half-dead and chained. As she rushes for the telephone, a portrait draws her gaze—goodness gracious, it's her, but in what an unusual rig-out! At that moment, her mother's murderer creeps up from behind and greets her with these words: 'The thirsty animal makes its way to the drinking hole!' The repulsive fellow threatens her with a pistol to which Nadia–Madhuri reacts astonishingly calmly. She simply waits for the right moment to sweep the pistol from the criminal's hand in such a refined manner that her companion, a German shepherd dog, can catch the weapon in his mouth. Pugnacious, she hurls an elaborate vase at her tormentor with all her might. In the meantime, however, many other men have crawled out of the mysterious house with its revolving doors: the criminal's entourage.

Nadia–Madhuri fights the crooks in the tried-and-tested manner with relish, lifts one of them high up, throws the next one into the dirt and delivers a multitude of hooks to the chin. This wrangling is observed from the street by several men driving by. 'Is that a woman?' one of them asks his companion in astonishment. 'Sexy thing!'—and with this comment the gentlemen rush to Nadia–Madhuri's aid, by which time she's finished up herself. Nonetheless, she thanks them with well-bred politeness and leaves the courtyard—without giving away her name. A short while later she is back home, stretched out on the sofa with her splendidly waved coiffeur.

Then the viewer discovers what's going on in the mysterious house. In that very place, the father of the twin sisters is being kept prisoner—a broken, helpless old man in chains. But that's not all: his wife's murderer has thought out a particularly sordid method of torture as revenge for his ruined life, especially thought out for the man he holds responsible for his misery. With shiningly polished shoes, the kidnapper presses down on a lever which opens a blind, rendering visible a one-way reflective pane of glass. At first glance, the scene now showing seems like a cinema screen on a cinema screen. And there, against a painted full-moon backdrop dances Nadia–Rani, the kidnapped twin sister, his beloved daughter! 'I'd rather be blind!' moans the despairing father at this sight. What at first seems like harmless scenery around a dancer, gradually transpires, as shown by the on-the-spot camera, to be a secret brothel. Beyond the revolving walls—the father hidden on one side, an office on the other—poker is being played, and smoking, gambling and drinking is rife. Nadia–Rani, it begins to dawn on the audience, is not merely an artiste in this establishment. Soon, she leaves the stage area and sashays barefoot in her dark sari among the tables. She leans lasciviously over each and every brothel visitor, her hands—in close-up—beckoning invitingly. So the kidnapper of her father, the murderer of her mother is Nadia–Rani's pimp, and from the little girl he has created a prostitute!

There is no dearth of insinuation in this scene. And yet the cliché of the actress/dancer as a prostitute is broken on a higher level of abstraction. The blonde Nadia–Rani may dance with a certain elegance, but she repeats the single movements over and over without resolving them according to Indian dance rules. Thereby, the scene comes across almost as a travesty of the usual cinematic arts of seduction. This cinematic depiction of prostitution seems to be more of a carnival-esque experiment, as Nadia's resolving of the conflict would also indicate.

Disguised as a man, complete with turban, tailcoat, moustache and spectacles, Nadia–Madhuri gains entry to the brothel for a second time and mingles with the guests. Nadia–Rani starts performing straightaway—this time she shows the guests a racy American tap-dance number with fencing interludes, dressed in a trouser-suit with geometrical appliqué. The good sister watches her wayward twin with the expression of a strict Latin teacher. This cross-dressing performance gives rise to further complications: from now on Nadia–Madhuri's suitor naturally confuses the brave, good blonde with her prostitute sister Rani. This turbulent confusion reaches its climax when Nadia–Madhuri clambers up the outside wall of the brothel and—this time in sari and pumps—squeezes through the window of her twin sister's dressing room. At gunpoint, the good sister forces the bad sister to change her costume. Bound and gagged, Nadia–Rani has to listen as her twin sister suggests a plan to get rid of her in a bizarre live murder show. With conspiratorial relish, the 'good' sister explains the details to the pimp/killer present. In the early hours of the morning, when the guests are drunk enough, Nadia–Rani (now being mistaken for the good sister) will end up on stage as 'the virgin, cut in two'. A famous magician's masterpiece would camouflage the brutal killing. At the appropriate time, a suitable barrel is rolled on to the stage. As the tension mounts, the police arrive unexpectedly. In a dramatic confrontation between the pimp/kidnapper and the two sisters, Nadia–Rani eventually sacrifices herself selflessly for Nadia–Madhuri and dies as a remorsefully happy sister in front of everyone.

It would be wrong from several perspectives to regard the moral of *Muqabala* from the resolution of the story alone. Wadia Movietone films were all productions targeting a mass audience and consequently the self-sacrifice of Nadia–Rani in the final minutes of the film can be viewed as a necessary tribute to the preferences of Indian cinema. A film in which the baddie doesn't die at the end is still today viewed in producers' circles as a certain flop. This is generally explained by the ancient Hindu theatre tradition. There's scarcely a person who would permit himself to disregard the dictum of the obligatory victory of good over evil in Indian cinema. In this respect, more notable than the unavoidable death at the film's conclusion is the almost burlesque way with which Fearless Nadia plays with the clichés that are closely entwined with the job of an actress.

Even if events in this film may give rise to the impression that this is a comedy through and through, it should be stressed at this point that *Muqabala* is regarded as an early 'masala' film. This typically Indian mix lines up extremely heterogeneous elements, the film alternating between genuine romance, expressive musical sequences, dramatic action and comedy numbers. And indeed Nadia–Rani plays the disreputable sister with all seriousness, if also with immense relish. In the brothel, where she has at least one man twisted round every finger and where she carries herself like a queen, she doesn't seem in the least disconsolate. As the good sister, on the other hand, she makes it apparent in each scene that as a woman she will reach her goal only if she unwaveringly goes her own way, independent from the weakly drawn men around her—be it in matters of the heart or family, in punch-ups or questions of clothing. Thus, the figure of Nadia in this film presents two female types, otherwise depicted as incompatible, coming surprisingly close to one another.

Moreover, with her entrance as a man, Nadia even dares an excursion into so-called 'gender bending'. Her disguise with the beard and turban may be understood as a satirical commentary on the male-dominated acting tradition, but is in any event a symbol of the considerable freedom that Fearless Nadia was granted by the cinema public of those days. Her screen personality was not only entitled to do all sorts of things usually reserved for men—she could also mingle with the brothel frequenters unrecognized and without having to cast off her guise at the end of the sequence and revealing herself as a woman.

Kisses, Flowers, Secrets

As a genuinely Western medium, during the silent-movie era, cinema offered the Indian public insights into the love and married life of foreign cultural circles with which Indians were largely unfamiliar until then. At the beginning of the sound film era, too, when the Indian film industry increasingly drove out foreign productions from the screen, Western films remained a source of inspiration and provided, indirectly at least, a confrontation with Indian customs and habits. Or, to put it more precisely: there were often downright provocations. A Western woman kissing a man on-screen was just about tolerated. Indian actresses abandoning themselves to such intimacies, however, caused a scandal. The aversion to acted eroticism was getting increasingly pronounced.

When in 1932, for example, the director Ezra Mir, fresh back from Hollywood, told the story of a beautiful gypsy girl with a passion for rich men in *Zarina*, he had his lead actress Zubeida kiss her screen partner Jal Merchant in a close-up. This scene kicked up a proper uproar in Lahore: the incensed audience threatened to burn down the cinema if the film was not immediately taken off the programme. Public exchange of intimacies—as is said even today—is simply not part of Indian culture and is an affront to the viewer. Yet, this contempt for eroticism in Western films in no way led to an axeing of love scenes in Indian cinema. Hand in hand with the censors' regulations, the last few decades have brought a completely independent erotic vocabulary of metaphors, symbols and situations that is generally viewed as kitsch in the West and is often misunderstood.

Romantic love as a precursor to marriage tends to be an alien concept within Indian society—at most it presents itself after the families of the bride and groom have agreed upon the compatibility of the arranged union. Since the possibilities of pre-marital get-togethers between man and woman are extremely limited in real life and are heavily ritualized, much takes place in the imagination of the individual, an imagination that knows and cultivates a collective imagery drawn from popular cinema. In this, the meeting of young Krishna with a milkmaid is seen as the most important mythological source. In the guise of a cowherd, the god Krishna consorts with the young, languorous women in the midst of a pastoral landscape. Borne along by mutual attraction, a game of erotic hide-and-seek commences in this idyll to which the women abandon themselves just as much as the polygamous god, far from the restraints of society and without the burden of marital intentions.

Similarly liberated from cinematic reality or narration, the obligatory song inserts are in the nature of intermezzi in a poetic parallel universe. Hero and heroine pursue each other for the course of every song, dancing and singing in virginal landscapes, meeting in front of the fountain beneath the full moon, vanishing behind blossoming trees, white doves looking on as they caress each other briefly on the shoulder or the hand. This eternal foreplay attains a certain erotic directness in the lyrical song texts, but this is kept separate from the image. The actual kiss is always hidden at the last moment by roses unfurling on the screen or by suddenly tumbling waterfalls, and erotic fulfilment is banished to the realm of the imagination through the blurring of tender movements made by the couple. The relatively strict visual rules for love scenes in Indian cinema are a thorn in the eye of many progressive cinema experts in India because of their unrealistic and intellectually incomprehensible, allegorical structure, which to their mind is proof of the cinematic backwardness of the country. A representative of this faction recently asked a well-known director in a taunting undertone, 'How would you actually go about filming a love scene if there weren't any trees?'

For Nadia, such love scenes represented a certain problem, as her way of moving, of dancing and singing didn't correspond to what the public normally expected of a woman. To renounce them completely, however, was out of the question unless her producers were willing to risk a flop. Nadia's roles, in which she stood out primarily through her fighting and sporting talents, would also be at odds, in terms of her credibility, with the cinematic full-moon sort of romance. That is why the singing and dancing was often left to the supporting actresses.

At the same time, Nadia's popularity was also notable for her special sex appeal. While her often daring attire showed off legs, arms and torso in an unusually generous manner, her way of fighting was perceived as alternative satisfaction. In order for Nadia's powerful sexual presence not to come across as threatening or indeed immoral, there was always a man at her side acting as assistant and fellow in combat with whom she entertained a marginal romance. This mantel was so often taken up by the muscular John Cawas that the pair even made it into the

Limca Book of Records, an Indian equivalent of the *Guinness Book of Records*. No other Indian film couple were to be seen as often together on screen and scarcely any other man could have filled the space next to her.

The Wadia brothers' attention had been drawn to John Cawas when he was pictured in Indian newspapers in daring 'Mr Universe' poses and had achieved six unusual world records one after the other, such as, for example, deflecting a battering ram held by sixteen men with his stomach or balancing on his back a brand-new Chevrolet with four passengers. With such a partner, it was all the more necessary to ensure—with the utmost of care—that the balance of power between Nadia and John Cawas wasn't distorted in the few romantic scenes. Sitting on a park bench next to one another, a little distance had to be kept between them at all times, although she—in contrast to all other film ladies—always sat a little more to the fore or higher up than her partner in the chosen perspective. These peripheral liaisons with John Cawas or other stunt legends always seem like a concession that underlines Nadia's femininity without robbing her of her independence. In fact, they never culminate in a screen marriage; 'it simply wasn't necessary' says Homi Wadia. With this appeal, chaste and erotic at the same time, Fearless Nadia as a white woman was entering a socially explosive terrain in the 1930s and 1940s. It was an even more risky challenge for her than what her colleagues had to face as they walked the saint–whore tightrope.

Ever since the first Indian uprising against the British colonial power in the year 1857, it was a 'proven fact' amongst the English that Indian men would avail themselves of every opportunity to rape every white woman within reach. 1857 became a trauma for the British in India with incredible consequences. English women and children were henceforth guarded like rabbits from snakes, which, in turn, encouraged the grotesque isolation from their surroundings adopted by the British women themselves. It was considered perverse and disrespectful of their own race if English people got 'too involved' with Indian men or women and the British government tried for their part to prevent 'mixed marriages'. But it was only the official Indian England that functioned this way. Off the record, the British colonial community indulged in an extremely steamy, erotically charged sub-culture beneath the prudish surface. There was much drinking and flirting, for the heat and the boredom could scarcely be borne otherwise. Moreover, India was a marriage market for the 'fishing fleet', that is to say ladies from England who were hard to marry off, and who hoped to find a husband amongst the less choosy bachelors in the empire. Along the way, however, many of them came to acquire a dubious air as they travelled to hill stations and their more pleasant climes (Simla being the most popular destination) in the hot months. The grass widows enjoyed themselves at garden parties where one could retire for the space of a dance or two to so-called 'kala jagas' or darkened corners, beyond divans cushioned with flowers and ferns. In Simla, there was even a hotel that provided the special service of an early bell that was rung in time to give each guest the chance to wake up in the right bed. Professional prostitutes avoided Simla on principle: they didn't want to get embroiled with amateurs.

Like the actresses in Western films, English women in India remained unapproachable, alien, distant, rich, immoral, seductive and often also hated. Nadia was the only actress who looked like a memsahib and yet was an Indian. She acted in Indian films but her roles didn't fit to the existing categories of ideal film-wives, submissive film-daughters or devilish prostitutes. Nadia operated in a blind corner, so to speak, whose erotic tension perhaps finds its best expression in the recollections of one of her fans, Khanderao Kelkar: 'We were forced to keep ourselves under control everywhere: at work, in the family, faced with our superiors, on the street, there was nowhere where we could give full rein to our emotions—apart from the cinema. There we could shout and laugh and cry without it being invasive or embarrassing. Everyone did it. And that is the reason too why the Nadia films were so popular because no other film managed to draw us in as much. Come the end of the film we were completely drained and exhausted, but at the same time there was magnificent relief, a catharsis.'

4
LADY IN THE DRIVER'S SEAT

Cover of programme booklet for Miss Frontier Mail

Nadia was an enthusiastic car driver both in real life and on the big screen. Her driving style underlined her personal character traits—swift, unafraid and independent—and impervious to all impediments life has to offer. Since Nadia's second successful film, *Miss Frontier Mail* (1936), her serene handling of the latest technical achievements was part of her star image. Now she could be seen tearing over the screen in smart convertibles, balancing on the roofs of hurtling trains or on the wings of shaky propeller-driven planes depending on the story. Like James Bond, Nadia's cinematic incarnation was capable of expertly using all manner of contemporary vehicles, electrical machines and spying devices. Because industrial development in India—and with it that of the history of cinema—took a different course to that of countries in the Western world, in her performances, Nadia had correspondingly different tasks to manage as regards modern technology than her stunt counterparts in Europe or the USA.

Historically, industrialization in India took anything but a regular course. While some areas of land have barely any developed infrastructure even today, back in 1864 the British colonial power had a railway line built that connected the cotton-growing area of Gujarat with Bombay. When the first locomotive thundered along the tracks it caused a sensation. Speaking about his own country folk and their incredulous reactions, K.N. Kabraji, a resident of Bombay, says:

> [...] most of them could not believe at first that this strange locomotive called the steam engine could be a product of human skill and science. They saw that no horses or bullocks were employed to draw

> the train and were convinced that the wonderful white man who could work other miracles had employed some demons or other invisible powers to draw so swiftly and easily the enormous load of wagons and carriages. There was no other way to account for this wonder and so they brought propitiatory offerings of coconuts to the unearthly power and were ready to worship it.[7]

Thirty-two years later, on 7 July 1896—there still wasn't a single car on the streets of Bombay—India's first cinema screening was advertised in fliers as the 'miracle of the century'. The *Times of India* announced the event as 'the greatest scientific discovery of our time!' The Lumière brothers had sent their assistant Marius Sestier to Bombay on his way to Australia with six film copies in his baggage. Among them was *The Arrival of a Train*. In this short documentary, a train rollicks towards the audience, resulting in zestful shock, and showing in a most impressive manner how cinema as a medium was itself both part of technical progress and at the same time its propagator from the beginning. The audience at the commencement of the century—for the most part excluded from the active use of the latest technology, and not only in India—participated emotionally in the achievements of modern civilization via the big screen. Just like with *Star Trek* or *Independence Day* today, people loved to be fascinated, frightened and amazed in the cinema.

The French writer Louis Aragon, for example, beautifully describes with what emotion he discovered his interest in cinema in the early Hearst Pathé film, *Perils of Pauline*: 'In

---

[7] Diwedi, Sharada and Rahul Mehrotra, *Bombay: The Cities Within*, Bombay: India Book House, 1995.

the film the personification of speed appears and Pearl White doesn't act to assuage her conscience, but rather for the sport of it. She acts for the sake of acting ... Who would dream of taking her seriously? Here, then, is the drama appropriate for our century!' His contemporary, the film critic Louis Delloc also hero-worshipped the blonde heroine Pearl White who went down in film history as the idol of soldiers in the First World War: '... this luscious heroine, the picture of health, without ulterior motives, her graceful power, her success ... Pearl White can do anything and does it so well she delights the audience. Leaving her films one is filled with an untrammelled desire to drive cars and fly aeroplanes, to horse-ride, to shoot like an ace, to dance, to ice-skate, to swim, to dive—to do everything, absolutely everything, and the gap's not wide between desire and its execution.' It was this very Pearl White who had enticed Fearless Nadia to the cinema again and again when she was still a schoolgirl: 'In *Perils of Pauline* I remember one sequence where Pearl drives a race car to save the hero from some spies. It was wonderful to see a woman driving such a fast car. In Bombay at that time there were not that many cars and even fewer women driving them. So it really inspired me to try it. Of course I was still too young and Mummy didn't have that kind of money. But in time when I could afford it I purchased as many cars as I liked. And I always remembered Pearl White. In fact, when J.B.H. Wadia decided to publicize me as the Indian Pearl White I was very flattered.'

The Daughter of Rolls Royce

In contrast to the Western world, access to modern gadgets and technological luxury is denied to the majority of the Indian population. It was no different in Nadia's day than now. Quite apart from the political and social injustice of this situation, people who know that they will never have the chance to partake of the multitude of machines and gadgets are compelled to nurture psychological defence mechanisms. These are of course successful to varying degrees in individual cases, but collective strategies may also be discovered—nowhere more than in cinema, for example, in the Fearless Nadia films.

Miss Frontier Mail, 1936

As the modern heroine of numerous stunt films, Nadia treats the fascination with technology with absolute respect, but at the same time she provides plenty of occasions to laugh at cars above all. An important example of this is her famous 'Rolls Royce Ki Beti' (the daughter of Rolls

Royce). The very name for the vehicle that only bears a distant similarity to the 'mother' is a typically ironic way of dealing with a symbol of technical superiority of the West, one that originates from the homeland of the colonial power of India to boot. 'Rolls Royce Ki Beti' appears in several of the Nadia films and developed a popular life of its own. The car had countless tricks: for example, as a rule 'she' only springs to life when Nadia delivers a kick to the body of the car, hardly ever reacting to the turning of the ignition keys. In *Lutaru Lalna*, Nadia even has the car jumping through the air with the result that public servants believe there is a demon in the 'Daughter of Rolls Royce' and pursue 'her'. And, of course, 'she' can drive without a driver and often uses this ability to pick up Nadia.

The stories surrounding the car with its human characteristics are examples of a strategy with which not only Nadia films but the popular films of India as a whole rebel against Euro-American civilization. Although Indian cinema is extremely influenced by Hollywood and European films, it is part of the nature of Indian films to make a caricature, to distort and imitate in such a way that something new and different emerges. The Indian film specialist Anil Saari believes that the modern Western way of living resembles the fairy-tale-like 'pot of gold at the end of the rainbow', the unattainable nature of which is felt not least as a psychological burden. In contrast to many Western productions that tend to increase this pressure, popular Indian films, according to Anil Saari, take the exotic and unattainable aspect of the Western way of life and exaggerate it into the realm of the fantastical, defamiliarize it or make a parody of it in such a way that no feelings of inferiority are evoked amongst the audience.

While poverty always has an elegant countenance in Indian film—an impoverished film heroine is, as a rule, beautiful, replete with perfectly coiffed hair and painted nails—wealth is depicted in almost symbolic denseness. The houses of the rich in Indian cinema are crammed full with the insignia of wealth to such an extent that the actors can barely move on the set. This more fantastical than realistic manner of narration and design in Indian films is a fundamental part of the cinema experience that distracts viewers from their desire for material items. 'Rolls Royce Ki Beti' is a typical luxury object, beyond dreams of possession, to be ogled with relish in the cinema. 'Don't you think,' one letter writer to the editor of *Filmindia* pens in November 1941, 'that Wadia's "Rolls Royce Ki Beti" would fetch a fabulous price in these days of petrol rationing? She seems to start with a mere kick!' The editor's response: 'Not with a mere kick. That box of tricks requires Nadia's kick and that kick costs Rs 1500/- a month.'

Nadia's stunt scenes with cars, trains and aeroplanes are all produced with great zest, and stretch far beyond the limits set by a realism-bound credibility. Nadia, however, for all her apparent fun behind the wheel keeps her mind firmly on her goal: she uses technology as a means to an end, to fight for justice, for what's good, to combat those who suppress the rights of others. The success of *Hunterwali* established her social attitude and it was henceforth retained as her major characteristic—fighting with unusual means, for the greater good, for the poor and those deprived of their rights. From this combination, a pattern emerged that is known in India as formula film. This speciality of Indian cinema describes a kind of temporary, cinematic recipe for success which actually tells the same story over and over again in variations until the audience wants something new.

Alongside a fixed dramaturgy prescribing precisely what sort of conflict shall be resolved in which way, and laying down time for song inserts, romantic interludes and slapstick, dramatic stunts were an integral part of a formula film with Fearless Nadia. For this, it was necessary to keep up with the technical standard of contemporary Western productions since in no other genre is this as important as in stunt films. This was an enormous challenge for Wadia Movietone as film technology in India was nowhere near as far advanced as, for example, in the USA. The quirky stories about 'Rolls Royce Ki Beti' were an element of the wide repertoire of tricks used by Wadia Movietone to successfully overcome the considerable disadvantages and remain more than capable of competing with Indian and Western stunt productions. Nadia, her directors, producers and special-effect experts developed a talent for improvisation both in front of and behind the camera that can perhaps only be properly appreciated today, decades after their evaluation in the cinemas. The passion with which the Wadia Movietone troupe produced one film after the other seems a privilege of those irretrievable years in which, every now and then, the actual film-making itself was more bizarre than what the viewers were shown on the big screen. In the heat of the moment, certain methods and tricks were used on which the dust had to settle a little before they could be spoken of outside the studio.

Secrets from the Bag of Tricks

How do you get an orang-utan to accept a film actress as a temporary partner? You place it on the passenger seat of the production car after film rehearsals and chauffeur it as an actor with equal rights to dinner together. And if by chance this is to be taken at the elegant Taj Mahal Hotel, the director must simply insist that the ape may avail itself of its bananas at the sought-after place next to its prominent colleague. For Homi Wadia, such arrangements constituted the easier part of his job, and to this day he loves unconventional behaviour of this sort.

The film business is an uncertain one. Every new production runs the risk of being a flop and according to what the film has cost, a single failed film can mean the bankruptcy of a studio. In contrast to his elder brother JBH, Homi Wadia as a born businessman was aware of this situation all through his long career. Today he can look back proudly on the 105 films of his own which had varying degrees of success but which never failed to recover their cost. As a director and producer, Homi was always more cautious than his brother, and preferred to play safe. He was extremely disciplined and worked effectively and economically. After *Hunterwali*, it was clear to him that this formula would work only as long as he managed to surprise his audience in every new film with a delightful ambience, stunts never before seen, and incredible special effects. And, according to popular opinion, it worked, as the memory of Nadia fan Girish Karnad proves:

> The boy who got the news first in our school was the hero of the day. Even as one entered the class, one sensed from the charged atmosphere that a stunt film was coming! Once this news was digested, we all prayed it would be a 'Nadia' or a 'Wadia' film (the words were deliciously interchangeable for us). As more details trickled in and the opening of the

film drew nearer, intimate plans were laid about how to break in through the inevitable crowds and get a place in the last row of the three-anna section.[8]

It was no different during the screening: as soon as Nadia was glimpsed on the screen for the first time, the people on the cheapest seats rose from the benches, clapping and cheering with enthusiasm. The viewers in the rather better four-anna seats had their view blocked by this and they yelled: 'Get down, you swine! Sit down now!'

In the lead-up to any new film, Homi Wadia looked to American productions for inspiration, all the more so when a film had experienced a successful run in the West and had been received well by the comparatively fewer Indians who watched American films. However, Homi's cinema visits weren't solely for non-material inspiration. Especially during later years, when budgets for producing stunts didn't grow commensurate with the rising expectations of the audience, expensive shipwrecks, aeroplane crashes and raging fires as could be seen in America would have remained wishful thinking for Homi if he hadn't known how to help himself very pragmatically. When he came across suitable special effects in a film that he could envisage as part of the next Nadia film, he made an appointment with an assistant, usually the faithful Ismail Shaikh. They would watch the last evening show of the relevant film in a good friend's cinema, usually the Alexandra Theatre, deep in the heart of Bombay's red-light district. The man allowed Homi's assistant access to the projection room during the showing. From there, the young man had to

[8] Karnad, Girish, 'Down Memory Lane: When "Stunt" was King', *Seventy Years of Indian Cinema*, 1985.

watch his boss through the small window during the course of the film. Homi tapped on the seat in front whenever a 'good' scene came up, the secret sign for the assistant to mark the place on the film roll with a piece of paper. With the knowledge of the cinema owner, after the show was over, the assistant brought the marked roll to the Wadia studio for the night where the American action scene was oh-so-quietly copied. The original film reel was back in the cinema punctually for the next screening the next day.

Yet, Homi Wadia was not yet satisfied with the method. Contrary to his brother JBH who—as a former lawyer—didn't like this kind of 'borrowing' for obvious legal reasons, Homi was more concerned about the signalling system. To his taste, it was too imprecise, as many metres of expensive celluloid were wasted. And so the technique was perfected. A little hole was drilled in the floor of the projection room through which a thread could be lowered. Homi Wadia now sat quite far back in the auditorium. Next to him hung the suspended thread attached to which was a small bell in the projection room. From then on the assistant stuck the pieces of paper in the running film roll almost down to the last second! Thus, a system was established that bequeathed many a dramatic moment to Nadia fans which otherwise would have been lost to them for reasons of cost.

The Man with the Magic Hands

These 'borrowed scenes', however dramatic, didn't in themselves add up to a film. It took 'magic hands' to integrate an American aeroplane accident or the sinking of a ship into a Nadia film. The machines and constructions necessary for doing so were simply not available for sale in India however. It called for a creative do-it-yourself talent coupled with technological film know-how. One young man had the necessary qualifications at his disposal, someone who had worked his way up in another studio from poster-painter to set designer: Babubhai Mistri. His nickname in those days was 'Black Thread' since it was this very method he employed to move furniture and shift walls as though with an invisible hand. This self-taught man was wooed to Wadia Movietone and was henceforth in charge of the much-praised attractions in their films. For this legendary trick master, Nadia was the goddess and mother of the studio, a one-off lady: courteous, disciplined, courageous like no other! It was pure pleasure to work with her and her co-fighters, and to think up all manner of things that made the impossible possible on the silver screen. For example, should a typhoon be the order of the day in a production, Babubhai Mistri built miniature models to fit what was on hand. This could be action clips from American films or original film locations in which the actors would eventually drown or burn or where aeroplanes would tumble from the skies. The team went to view waterfalls, dams or jungle locations before starting the trick filming to check whether filming would be possible without endangering life. Then Babubhai Mistri got down to making his models. It took ten to twelve days to build a model about three to four square metres in size, using a coconut palm as his means of measurement. Depending on its size, it was fitted with huts, rivers and mountains. At some point, this was flooded with water tanks, during which the typhoon was filmed by at least four specially prepared cameras. Because the trick master knew his model better than anyone, Homi Wadia left it to Babubhai Mistri to give Nadia precise directorial advice at the original location so that the finished film looked 'believable' when she vanished in a flood or grabbed the ladder of an aeroplane from the back of a galloping horse. Nadia was fabulous during these shots, accepting the riskiest of suggestions without grumbling or boasting, Babuhai Mistry recalls.

The real art consisted in taking the very heterogeneous material from foreign films, trick shots and original scenes, and making it fit together. With this aim in mind, Babubhai Mistri gradually availed himself of the entire varied palette of pre-digital era film tricks: with travelling mats he had Nadia fly through the air in a celestial carriage or leap on horseback over vast abysses; using double exposure, Nadia got a twin sister or shrunk to the size of a mouse in an encounter with a giant; a camera running backwards allowed Nadia to leap over walls metres high from a standing position with the greatest of ease. On the sound side, similar experiments were rife: the sound engineer Burjore Tata struck coconuts against the sun battery on the studio roof, producing a passable hoof-like noise, while the tiles in the gents' toilet were favoured for the romantic drumming.

The trick experts at Wadia Movietone knew exactly when the camera had to move a touch faster or slower to heighten the drama, to draw out the tension. Yet, in spite of it all, today they are all unanimous in their opinion that the success of all their experiments was no less thanks to the naivety of the audience of those days. It did not matter too much if something was wobbly, if in one sequence day and night scenes were mixed, provided the 'miracles' worked in favour of the heroine! Another Wadia Movietone employee Nanabhai Bhatt elucidated the innocence of the audience with the example of a sequence from *Hunterwali Ki Beti* in which Nadia was captured by nasty criminals. Standing in front of a barred window, she pondered how she could escape. As a woman of extraordinary strength it seemed appropriate that she should bend the bars and, according to the stage instructions, that is just what she did. But the scenery on hand was made of very cheap material with the result that Nadia not only bent the bars but brought down the whole wall. With a slightly uneasy feeling, the team decided against re-shooting the scene on grounds of expense. In the cinema, according to Nanabhai Bhatt, the audience reacted enthusiastically: 'Look how strong she is! She can even move walls!' The prerequisite for the high level of acceptance of such daring and not-always-perfect trick scenes was the excitement of the action, the responsibility of which rested most of all on the shoulders of the bold actors.

Nadia's Gangster Troupe

From the beginning of his career, Homi Wadia had preferred to surround himself with actors with advanced athletic and artistic abilities. Besides Nadia, these were men who courageously leapt from any rooftop, who felt at home on galloping wagons and could deliver punches with as much aplomb as they could take them. They were tough guys, characters that required a different kind of directing to that of, say, the classical lovers in a melodrama. As a stunt director, Homi Wadia placed emphasis on discipline that was only relaxed and reduced a peg or two after work in joking and fooling around with his circle of colleagues. Homi insisted that the fight scenes, the attacks and leaps planned for a film be rehearsed meticulously in the studio so as not to waste either time or material on location. This kind of thing could only be done with a warmed-up team about which Nadia reported: 'It was really hard work. And I don't mean just the filming itself. When we weren't filming we often worked even harder—on the training meadow. We trained, trained, and trained some more, we tried out new tricks, practised falling—everything, every day. I always referred to the others in the troupe as "all my little gangsters", one of them being Sayani, the baddie in the films—he was the first ever man I carried on my shoulders.'

For Homi, discipline was an indispensable tool to set in motion his cinematic talent for abstraction. Thanks to long years of experience, he already had the cutting order of the stunt scenes precisely in his head before filming began. He knew which wide shots he would later require in the film, which close-ups, which sequences of movement. This rare talent made him the best stunt director in India in the 1930s and 1940s. Time and again he was invited to other studios for guest engagements. But Homi Wadia declined such offers—he advised other directors, but worked solely for his own studio. Some of his early actors followed in his footsteps and come the end of their screen career became stunt directors themselves. Among them was Nadia's screen partner of many a year, John Cawas, who described the following incident during the filming of *Diamond Queen* (1940) as typical of Homi's working method. One day, an extremely dangerous scene was to be filmed at a waterfall down which Nadia and several other actors and extras were to hurl themselves. Everyone was afraid of the scene although all the actors were attached to ropes. It was slippery, the water was raging. All the actors spent the entire day in damp costumes. There was no time for lunch. Then it happened: one of the extras, a boy from the neighbouring village, slipped awkwardly, couldn't gain his balance, tumbled down, and hours later could only be assumed dead. The filming was stopped. The team returned to the studio, Homi Wadia offered his condolences to the family and tried to lessen their grief with a high compensatory payment.

The work on this film had already progressed very far and the waterfall scene could on no account be removed from the plot. The team appointed Nadia as spokeswoman with the task of persuading Homi to stop the film project. On account of the tragic incident, no stuntman wanted to jump down that waterfall now! Homi wouldn't waver from his course. With dismal premonitions, the team gathered at the location a few days later. What no one had guessed was that Homi had decided to take on the dangerous stunt himself. When he returned to the shore, wet and dripping after the successful shot, everyone was extremely impressed by his courage, some people even sinking to their knees in front of him.

Accidents were part and parcel of everyday life at Wadia Movietone. The only way to deal with the high-risk job was to make fun of it. Nadia was an expert at this, and managed to pull her colleagues' legs repeatedly. Her black humour was a quality that Homi Wadia particularly admired in Nadia. In response to the question why so many accidents occurred not only during filming but in the films themselves, he said: 'These sorts of accidents on-screen always bring pleasure to the audience, they are dramatic turning points and a popular method to have a hero lose his memory or a bad character die. Of course as a rule they are not real accidents. Although there are exceptions! In *Miss Frontier Mail* (1936) when Nadia is pursuing the villains in her Mercedes, she comes upon an unexpected street blockade. It was planned that she would race up to the wooden crates but would brake in time and discover that the villains are hiding in the bushes. But *Miss Frontier Mail* was one of her first films, and Nadia had just got her driving licence. She somehow lost control of the car and drove at full throttle into a tree, destroying the camera in passing. There was a terrible crash and we were all scared to death as we saw her lying hunched over the steering wheel. Fortunately, there was no front window! When we went over to her and asked if anything had happened to her, she looked at us for a moment in total confusion, almost with a crazed look in her eyes. The car was a write-off. Then she began to laugh: "Yes, something has happened. My bra is torn." I remember clearly how that evening, Nadia insisted on driving home herself. "I have to overcome my fear," she explained. "Madame Astrova taught me never to give in to a fright, to face it and break it."'

The Woman with No Double

Nadia was the first Indian actress to work without a double and to perform all her own stunts. Wadia Movietone advertised this and all her fans knew it. This fact was so integral to her fame that even sixty years on only a few people in the know admit that there was a 'helper' every so often. Especially in scenes in which Nadia had to swing on vines or chandeliers. In contrast to the riding, fighting, fencing and swimming, these scenes often didn't work particularly well with her and so it was up to an actor by the name of Raja Sandow to disguise himself as Nadia on occasion. In the freeze frame, a very thin man can be spotted sporting a blonde wig with enormous breasts made of hard balls attached to him. It was apparently not as easy to imbue the legs with Nadia's stature, leading to a terribly grotesque physique. It is not hard to imagine the ridicule the Wadia troupe showered on this doppelgänger. A proud and certainly vain person, Nadia had no choice but to laugh along with them so that her dignity and position wouldn't be endangered. What else could she have done?

Hunterwali attributed a role to her as an actress that insisted she constantly prove herself an equal match in strength for any man, in the studio and on the big screen. The steely determination with which she addressed these expectations is shown by the unified reports of erstwhile colleagues who claim they never witnessed Nadia weak, afraid or overwhelmed during filming. If something didn't work, she laughed as though all this filming wasn't terribly important at all. Homi Wadia, her director and after their third or fourth film together also her lover, tried to hide the discreetly lived relationship with his lead heroine behind his decidedly equal treatment. Sometimes Homi shooed her around just as relentlessly as the other actors, one former colleague recalls. From time to time, he downright harried her when it came to embarking upon risky situations and didn't spare her in any way.

This method of working drove even the constantly cheerful Nadia to the edge of her capabilities at times: 'From the moment of carrying Sayani around in *Hunterwali*, Homi continually had me hoisting men onto my shoulders. However, carrying a man is nothing compared to heaving a calf around! I had to do a scene like that for the film

Bambaiwali. A calf is an astonishingly wobbly, slippery and extremely floppy animal to carry. According to the stage directions I was to have a very serious, calm and confident expression on my face as I carried the calf on my shoulders. I found that incredibly difficult because the creature struggled like mad and dug its hooves painfully into my chest. At the end of the scene, I was in tears and couldn't take any more.' With Sayani as her villain and opponent, Nadia put up with numerous tricky situations. For *Diamond Queen*, the pair of them were supposed to fight furiously in an open coach that was racing up a steep road. The scene was rehearsed a couple of times successfully. During filming, however, the brakes stopped working and the coach raced towards the vertical drop before the curve. Sayani, Nadia reported, was screaming at the top of his voice. 'I shouted back to hold on tight but he was seized by panic and jumped out. He broke his ankle because of it. I'd stayed in the coach that came to a halt at the cliffs. Not exactly a gentle landing, but I was unscathed.'

Miss Frontier Mail

The Wadia Movietone team worked in the knowledge that they were the best in their field in India. That fired their ambition and Nadia's too. As such they did not have to be persuaded much to conduct an experiment for their next big success after *Hunterwali*: the railway thriller *Miss Frontier Mail* which came in 1936. From the silent movie era on, the Wadia brothers discovered in the railways what was cinematically a powerful and effective method of transport. It seemed natural to replace Nadia's horse with a train. *Miss Frontier Mail* is the story of the conspiracy of a villainous aeroplane company to rob the railway of its customers by causing murderous train crashes. Nadia plays Savita, the daughter of a railway stationmaster unjustly accused of murder. She exposes the spy ring and, after a series of wild chases, prevents the murder of many innocent rail passengers. The main attraction was certainly the fighting on the top of moving trains.

To begin with, Nadia was dismissive of the project because, in her opinion, this was really going too far. But her male colleagues, with railway film experience under their belts, just laughed at her. This was typical of the work environment at Wadia Movietone, where everyone egged everyone else with sporting ambition on to new heights and got a kick out of it. True to her motto of trying anything once, Nadia finally did climb on to the roof of a train. The level area on the carriage roof was dangerously narrow but Nadia grew so accustomed to the lofty climes that after a few days of filming she didn't even come down for lunch. That didn't make the whole undertaking any less foolhardy, however. Even today, one can only watch with heart-stopping wonder as Nadia, in her elegant white tennis outfit, darts across the roof of the thundering train, chasing her murderous enemies from carriage to carriage and niftily leaping over the gaps in between. It is hard to believe that these scenes were filmed on real trains with no particular safety measures in place! For filming purposes, Homi Wadia had rented a train from the siding of a coal pit in the district of Borivili: five goods wagons, one passenger carriage and the engine. The resulting shots were so realistic that the railway company wouldn't allow the name of their famous train—in which Nadia had travelled as a schoolgirl to Peshawar—

to be used as the title of the action-filled film. Wadia Movietone inserted a 'Miss' in front of the name and notified the viewers in the credits that 'on no account was *Miss Frontier Mail* to be confused with the "Frontier Mail" train'!

Apart from cars, aeroplanes and railways, a secret radio station plays an important role as a technical attraction in *Miss Frontier Mail*. For today's viewer, the machine with all its bells and wires and microphones appears more comical than anything else, especially when the head of the aeroplane company (played by the ever-villainous Sayani) appears with it behind a plywood rail bridge. As the mysterious 'Signal X', Nadia's adversary keeps control over his alcohol-swilling repulsive band of villains via this very machine with its loudly crackling 'peep-peep-peep'. With her convertible, tennis racquet and a delicate lady's revolver, Nadia is clearly at a technical disadvantage. She makes up for these limitations with her physical qualities, in particular her fantastic speed that earns her the title of 'the Whirlwind' in the film. Coupled with her cleverness and refinement, she conquers the technology of the other side. She never allows herself to be intimidated by the brutal methods and instruments of the aeroplane company; she is ready to cope with the challenges of modern times. This particular character trait allows those in the audience who long to be part of the industrial progress to identify with her. It is noticeable that for the most part she avoids verbal arguments; her dialogues are kept to the bare minimum. She is represented primarily as a woman of action. Her lack of ability to speak in Hindi, initially viewed as a handicap by the Wadia brothers, quickly crystallizes on-screen into an advantage. 'The single most memorable sound of my childhood,' Girish Karnad recounts, 'is the clarion clear "Hey-y-y-y-y" as Fearless Nadia, regal on her horse, her hand raised defiantly in the air, rode down upon the bad guys. To us school kids of the mid-1940s, Fearless Nadia meant courage, strength and idealism.' The 'hey' became a Nadia trademark, like her mask and whip, and just like her laugh was often blended into the soundtrack post-filming.

On Risks and Side Effects

In the 1930s, Girish Karnad, then a teenager, was a typical Nadia admirer but being the offspring of a highly esteemed family, he was also an outsider to the fan community. The majority of Nadia's fans consisted of the illiterate working class. Men especially favoured films that bore the unofficial 'stamp of quality' whereby sisters could not be taken to the screenings. This referred mostly to the happenings on-screen but also to incidents that could occur in the cinema during the screening. Nadia fans loved to be caught up with her films in an almost dramatic manner which upper-class society was prone to look down upon as downright plebeian. Such enthusiastic demonstrations would be tolerated in their children only to a certain degree. Girish Karnad and his brothers and sisters were permitted to watch only one stunt film in the cinema every six weeks because otherwise the effect would have been almost unbearable for the parents: 'After watching the ['Nadia–John Cawas'] film at a matinee, our entire gang had to re-enact the stunt scenes by throwing punches at each other to the accompaniment of sounds like "dhum" and "ttho". Mother had strictly forbidden us to come anywhere near the living room after a stunt movie, since an obligatory part of this re-enactment was to roll across a table or a chair and take that piece of furniture crashing to the floor. So our scenes had to be "locationed" in the garden, which was not too comfortable. According to the tenets of the stunt film, a person hit squarely on the chin had to fly backwards, landing ideally either in a skylight or a chimney. Climbing a tree backward in simulation of this movement was not easy and could be hazardous.'

It was also in the interest of the cinema owners for children and young people to get the film out of their system like this after the showing. If newspaper reports of the time are to be believed, every showing carried the risk of the cinema being torn to bits by the audience in the throes of their enthusiasm. Thus, *Filmindia* warned Indian cinema owners in January 1938: 'Don't book a silly stunt picture and spoil the taste of your patrons. Rather close the cinema for some days. Your overheads thus accrued will not be greater than the ultimate loss you will suffer when the paying class of patrons will avoid going to your theatre, just because it is packed with the scum of the local population. Stunt pictures, as we find them in India today, are only seen by the lower class with no intelligence.'

Naturally, you could make good money with these films—in spite of all the prophecies of gloom. And the Wadia brothers knew this as well as any other professional in the film business. In October 1939, for example, Khwaja Ahmad Abbas reported on the craze for cinema in a northern Indian town where he had spent his holiday. In conversation with the 'cinema wallahs', the owners of travelling cinemas, Abbas discovered that more than half of the 25,000 inhabitants of Panipat—'illiterate people with low standards'—had been driven to financial ruin through an excess of watching films. Such news items horrified the conservative intellectuals and brought hefty critics into the arena. 'But,' said Abbas, 'one need not quarrel with these pious critics of the cinema. Their counterparts of an earlier generation objected to railways, steamers, motorcars, telegraphs and telephone. In time they will get used to the cinema, too.'

An Indian letter writer from Durban, South Africa, chimed in. By the end of the 1930s, Nadia films were being distributed as far away as that. This filmgoer wanted to know from the *Filmindia* editor in August 1939, what sense there was in Wadia Movietone producing films that were nothing but cheap entertainment and 'completely unnatural'. Baburao Patel replied: 'If you see the Wadia balance sheet at the end of the year, you will realize that the Wadias have a lot of commercial sense, which earns good money. Do you know that Wadia Movietone is one of our really financially sound companies? Wadias may not help Art but they do help themselves. An industry needs all sorts of people for it to be called an industry. And yet, I wish that the Wadias, with their huge resources, had taken a turn for good social pictures.'

5

FAMILY BUSINESS

Nadia and Homi Wadia, 1950

One day in autumn 1938, Homi and J.B.H. Wadia were asked to a meeting by a solemn-faced M.B. Billimoria, the business director. Billimoria, who had brought the first Wadia thriller *Thunderbolt* to the cinema and had then entered the business as part-owner, was the venerable and distinguished visage of the studio. For him it was a particularly uplifting moment when he laid the new balance sheets in front of the brothers: the figures showed that Wadia Movietone had become the number one film studio in Bombay.

This success was primarily a result of the income from the Fearless Nadia films, for the production of which an army of 600 studio hands were employed. The Wadia distribution net spanned the enormous Indian subcontinent and had undergone a considerable international expansion. Fearless Nadia was a name that functioned like a magnet in the whole Arab world, drawing people to the cinema. Her image was to be seen on the facades of countless film theatres from Beirut to Athens, Nairobi to Cape Town. Wadia Movietone had created a world star in Nadia—yet the Indian newspapers ignored this success as did the self-appointed judges of culture who laid down what good Indian film was. With raised eyebrows and slightly nauseated by the vulgar hurly-burly at Nadia showings, the cultural elite made no effort to acknowledge these films with their peculiarities and their charms. The secret of Nadia's success was snobbishly put down as violence-glorifying action entertainment that satisfied the baser instincts of the masses. This countrywide assessment of being an idol of the proletarian masses wasn't without its consequences on Nadia's life beyond the world of cinema. Because, in their private lives, the Wadia brothers were at home in precisely these circles that couldn't muster enthusiasm for their cinematic successes.

By 1939, Homi Wadia had directed five Nadia films—*Hunterwali*, *Pahadi Kanya*, *Miss Frontier Mail*, *Lutaru Lalna* and *Punjab Mail*. The director and his lead actress had an almost daily opportunity of getting to know each other better. Filming, with all its tensions, its moments of triumph, setbacks, irritations, and instances of happiness, is a professional activity conducive like no other for loving or hating one's colleagues. During this time, a fondness had sprung up between Nadia and Homi that was gradually blossoming to love. As far as all social duties went, Homi, a very shy and private man, preferred to stay in the shadow of his eloquent brother. So it fell to Nadia to take the initiative in making something more of the mutual liking. This attitude was not only unusual, it was seen as downright reprehensible for an Indian woman to take an active role in a relationship. That's why in the official version of their love story which appeared in film magazines years later, Nadia described it as a love-at-first-sight relationship.

Adapting to the tradition of Indian film star romances, she claimed that Homi had fallen in love with her when he looked through the lens of the camera for the first time. She had flashed just the briefest of smiles, and it had happened. In whatever manner the affair may have unfolded, the two of them had found one another at the end of the 1930s. And therein lies a story that's the stuff of Indian melodramas: man and woman discover great love but cannot marry as social convention, their caste, or religious affiliation dictate otherwise. On-screen, in contrast to almost all her colleagues, Nadia had nothing to do with such problems. She made up for it with gusto off screen.

An Eccentric Lot

The Wadia brothers hailed from a Parsi family. The Parsis form one of the oldest religious communities in the world and recognize the prophet Zarathustra as their founding father. Originally, the Parsis came from Persia where the Greek historian Herodotus visited them in the sixth century BC. He enthused about their honesty and their remarkable openness towards foreign traditions and customs. 'All pleasures and delights that they encounter, they adapt themselves,' wrote the historian, charmed. In the year AD 624, as Islam aggressively advanced towards Persia, most of the Parsis fled to tolerant India. As they were considered good, trustworthy business people, they were granted refuge there on condition that they wouldn't act as missionaries and wouldn't marry outside their own religious community. These strict rules of separation from the Indian population influenced the life of Parsis in exile over the centuries, and to this day non-Parsis are not allowed to enter their temples, in which fire is worshipped as the purest of all the elements. At the same time, this religion is characterized by a secular rationality of which the famous legend of their arrival in India is an example. At the first meeting between the Parsis and the king of the country, Sanjan, the latter asked for a glass of milk to be brought. 'Our country is like this glass of milk, it is full,' the king is purported to have said. At which point the oldest Parsi priest flipped a coin into the glass without spilling a drop and compared the Parsis to the coin that no one would notice. 'That's all very well, but the hospitality of our country can't be bought with money,' responded the king. Now the Parsi priest added a little sugar to the milk and said: 'Your Highness, just as the sugar sweetens the milk, so will we strive to sweeten your life through our activity.'

Parsi religion preaches a personal responsibility that binds individuals to one ethic above all others, one that is encapsulated in the simple maxim 'good thoughts, good words, good deeds'. Absolute honesty and social engagement carry more significance than fervent displays of religious feeling. The most striking characteristic of this religion, however, is the peculiar funeral rites that rarely go unmentioned in a Bombay novel and never in a travel guide. Since fire and earth are holy to the fire-worshipping Parsis, neither may be sullied by the impurity of the dead human body. As such, bodies of the Parsis who have died are taken to the 'Towers of Silence' on Malabar Hill and left to the feasting of the vultures.

The Parsis in today's Bombay make jokes about the funeral rites, even though they pay their last respects to a deceased relative with as much decorum as anybody else. Funeral rites may seem unusual material for the jokes of a people threatened with extinction (there are only an estimated 50,000 Parsis in Bombay) but this sense of humour, irony or self-mockery is a very characteristic trait of the community. J.B.H. Wadia's memoirs are full of incidents that are variants of the following Parsi self-projection: if there are three Parsis in a room, there are four arguments. But what does a Parsi do if he is left alone? He argues with the mirror.

The Wadia Family, 1961

The Wadia name carries with it responsibility, for an ancestor was one of the founding fathers of the town of Bombay. In 1735, Lovji Nusserwanji, a foreman at the East India Company's shipyards, was given the task of building ships in Bombay and modernizing the shipyards. Under Lovji's direction, the protected east side of the urban peninsula was gradually developed into a functioning harbour area and an attractive port of call for international shipping traffic. In Lovji's wake, more and more Parsis, numerous business people among them, settled in Bombay. They were attracted by the general social environment, which was much more liberal when compared to other regions and towns of India. The arrival of Lovji and five family members was to transform Bombay into one of the most significant harbour towns of Asia. As a token of thanks for his achievements, Lovji was awarded the title 'Wadia'—'Master Shipbuilder'—and was presented with several plots of land, among them large parts of the now millionaire quarters of Malabar. The grandfather of J.B.H. and Homi Wadia, Bomanjee Wadia, was the last one to work as a master shipbuilder for the East India Company. His descendants brought honour to the family name in other areas. Homi and J.B.H. Wadia buying back the former family seat Lovji Castle in Bombay's leafy Parel district as their studio space with the first profits of their film work speaks for itself. They referred to their unusual history through the selection of a sailing ship as their studio emblem. Like the roaring lion announcing MGM films, this emblem at the start of every Nadia film was a promise of an adventure to the audience.

The Parsi origin and the Wadia name brought some advantages to the studio, especially in the early days. Many doors open as if by magic, still today, to members of this highly respected family. Moreover, the brothers profited from being able to move more freely and being more flexible in culture, religion, and eating habits than Hindus or Muslims. It was natural to employ plenty of Parsis as co-workers, who were similarly open-minded and liberal. However, it was extremely important, particularly to J.B.H. Wadia as an agnostic, that one's origins and religious beliefs didn't play any role in the everyday workplace. Without this progressive climate, the integration of Nadia into the studio as a white actress performing lots of tasks traditionally allotted to men would scarcely have been possible. Private life was another matter.

Nadia was a Catholic, an actress, a stunt queen and on top of that suspected to be the mother of a child born out of wedlock. This made her the most unsuitable wife imaginable for Homi Wadia—at least from the perspective of family members with clout. Homi Wadia saw no other alternative but to keep his affair secret. His love for Nadia was not only extremely complicated regarding the prospect of a shared future, it also brought the unresolved conflicts of past years and the brotherly competition painfully to the surface once again. Homi Wadia's entry to the film world had been different, but no less complicated than that of his intellectual brother. As a little brother full of admiration for his older sibling, Homi had become infected at an early age by JBH's cinema fever. While still at school, Homi spent time every afternoon with his brother in his film laboratory as an enthusiastic assistant and knew from an early age that his future lay with cinema. As studying had never been a source of pleasure to him anyway, he didn't want to go through the trauma of the graduation exam as he revealed to his perplexed family one day. All the hue and cry didn't help, and the somewhat stubborn Homi messed up his exam out of pure contrariness. As a surrogate father, JBH felt somewhat responsible for the disaster. School pedagogues and wise Parsi family advisers were consulted, until finally a form of pedagogical blackmail was settled upon. On condition that Homi repeats the year and successfully passes the exam, JBH promised to make the younger brother a junior partner. With much ado and familial theatrics, this worked out. But in contrast to JBH who had freed himself from the demands of his family, Homi remained traumatized by the experience for many years.

The Complex Circle of Women Around Homi

Homi was particularly close to his mother; among his circle of acquaintances he was even known as a real mamma's boy. The Parsi psychologist Sheera Dastor claims that Parsi mothers are renowned for their 'overprotectiveness'. They spoil their children terribly but leave them no freedom to do what they want. It's hard to tell how true this stereotype was for Homi's mother, Dhunmai. At any rate, her strong distaste for the film business had an effect on Homi—he was plagued by a guilty conscience. The overwhelming success of his directing abilities didn't alter this. He had disappointed Dhunmai so much through his chosen professional path that under no circumstances did he want to impose his marriage to Nadia on her.

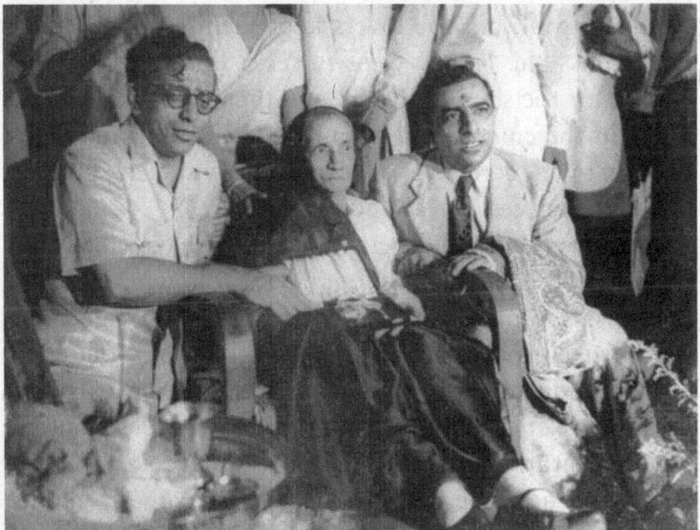

Mother Dhunmai with JBH and Homi

It wasn't only Homi's mother who railed against his liaison with Nadia. His two elder sisters, Gaimai and Soonamai, thought likewise—to them the family's reputation was of more concern than the contentment of their brother. Homi lived with one of these two ladies, and she spared no effort in introducing her brother to suitable young women. One of them was called Homai Golwalla, a charming young Parsi, whom Homi liked immensely. Had he married her, all the insurmountable difficulties would have been swept from the world, his mother would have been happy—a tempting prospect, indeed. Especially in the light of the exquisite nightlife in Bombay, with its intoxicating parties and countless dance events which drew the movers and shakers of society into the splendid Taj Mahal Hotel, not to mention the theatre premieres! Naturally, Homi spent many evenings with Nadia as well, but the lovers kept themselves hidden as far as possible. If they went to see a film together, they waited for the show to begin, and then crept in when the lights in the cinema had dimmed. Their affair may have been an open secret in gossiping Bombay society, but they avoided unnecessary attention.

Whatever course the evening had taken, Homi and Nadia would meet each other without fail the following morning, in the safety of the studio where their proximity was legitimized through their common work. And no one could hold a candle to her there. One wouldn't necessarily have described Nadia as a beauty in the classical sense, but her regular features flirted with every camera take. And her laugh and her blue eyes, framed by the superb, blonde head of hair did the rest. Homi was torn back and forth between studio and family, between expectations and inclination—a classical double bind situation he settled into without looking for a solution. Nadia, who after a very unsettled childhood and youth had yearned for a stable relationship for a long time, played along with the nerve-racking game out of necessity. But she had too much zest for life to let her uncertain future render her continually down or depressed.

This is also how the adult Haidee, the film-crazy daughter of J.B.H. Wadia remembers Nadia. As a small girl she spent happy afternoons with Nadia in the large expanse of the studio. When the filming schedule allowed, Nadia played with Haidee who enjoyed the privilege of being permitted to watch Nadia train at her riding or fencing whenever she pleased. Haidee, to whom the romantic ties between Homi and Nadia were not disclosed, had no idea that she could be related to Nadia in any way. To begin with, there was no trace of connection obvious to her. Nadia was never part of the party when the Wadias had excursions to the beach on weekends, and she gave family celebrations a wide berth. So for many a year Nadia was simply a grown-up friend to Haidee, until from certain observations Haidee put two and two together. Haidee's aunts occasionally got very worked up about Nadia supposedly being seen in the company of a handsome marine officer. Typical actress! Nadia and sailors, full stop: that was a gossip column in itself! Meanwhile, a different problem was developing with Bobby. He was a teenager now and his existence was an unspoken scandal. As these stories were discussed simultaneously in the same breath as Homi's eventual marriage, Haidee eventually understood what was going on. She, however, knew that her father, JBH, was the only member of the family pushing her uncle Homi to marry Nadia.

J.B.H. Wadia for his part had married a particularly beautiful Parsi by the name of Hilla Patell, an offspring of the 'Patells of Paris'. They were a dream couple in the eyes of Dhunmai, too, who was extremely proud of JBH for his choice of daughter-in-law. There is a photo of Hilla from the late 1930s, where she is posing in a black swimming costume. This amateur photo reveals through its very private, peripheral character that this lady was effortlessly confident, feminine and elegant in every situation. At first sight she seems to belong more to the Paris of the 1960s. Indeed, Hilla loved Paris. The bohemian French writer Colette was her great role model. Hilla had only a normal school education, but she was an enthusiastic reader of historical works, books on Judaism and above all biographies of artists. Throughout her life she continued to educate herself discreetly. She also knew how to preside over a household. Overlooking the Arabian Sea, the 'Casa da Vinci' was a villa furnished in a modern style, which hosted a number of famous figures, artistes and politicians. At the same time, Hilla was a welcome addition to the pleasure-seeking high society of Bombay in the 1930s and 1940s.

Hilla took an active interest in events at the studio, at the insistence of her husband, eleven years her senior. Their first-born son Vinci spent his infancy on silk cushions in a 'real' prince's cradle, once used as a prop in the Wadia Movietone films. Hilla regularly went with her daughter Haidee after school to Lovji Castle and took her place at her husband's side. In his memoirs, JBH dedicates a long postscript to his wife. In her he had found a confidante, and a very clever woman with whom he could discuss his screenplays at length. Lots of ideas were thanks to her. Hilla's involvement with the Wadia Movietone films wasn't restricted to her discreet presence in the studio or the evening reading sessions in the living room at home. She was always present when the plan for the daily filming was drawn up and JBH prized her criticism. Homi, close in age to his sister-in-law, didn't like this way of working at all. He viewed Hilla's constant presence in the studio as inappropriate meddling in the business concerns, endured by his brother out of blind love. According to JBH, Hilla's particular talent lay in set design—and she was the only person at Wadia Movietone with whose interference set designer Pestonji put up. It would have been natural for this fashion-conscious lady to discuss the costumes as well. Yet, wrote JBH, she didn't get involved in this area: 'Hilla was never really satisfied with the manner in which our actors were dressed. In particular she often found the clothing of our actresses too showy, too garish and loud. But she was smart enough never to get mixed up with this; at the end of the day the people wearing the clothes seemed to really like them. It's only in retrospect that I realise how right she was.' When one discovers that Nadia was primarily in charge of her own wardrobe, one guesses from this observation the abyss that existed between these two powerful women.

Not only in appearance were the black-haired, willowy Hilla and the corpulent blonde Nadia the embodiment of an explosive antagonism. Hilla liked being the centre of attention and perceived Nadia as a threat, as competition—despite the fact that JBH worshipped and admired his wife. This had more to do with the fact that the family's position in society had become somewhat unstable with the onset of Nadia's star status. Since *Hunterwali*, the studio—and with it the family—had to a certain degree become dependent on a woman who, with her dubious image and as the heroine of the proletarian masses, was endangering the family's reputation. These fears were stoked not least by the press. Baburao Patel for one liked to rub salt in this wound. For example, just at the time when Wadia Movietone had become the most successful studio in Bombay, Patel reported on an important political debate on film. JBH was also present at the gathering but Patel did not write about his contribution or opinion. All he commented was that J.B.H. Wadia had been present 'wielding a whip' and that 'no further comment' was necessary about his presence. The former lawyer and literature scholar couldn't be discredited in a meaner way. Such targeted digs at JBH were Patel's speciality for years. Here is another sample: 'I recently met my old acquaintance Pramila. With a puffy red face, and red bloodshot, runny eyes she was rigged up like a tigress. She apologised and said she was on her way home and was coming from the Wadia studio where she was acting in a jungle thriller. Well, we're living in hard times, and you've got to get by somehow.'

Patel was influential in the film scene of Bombay, and tried again and again to get Wadia Movietone to move away from the stunt film genre. He probably wouldn't have attempted this with such intensity, if he hadn't known that J.B.H. Wadia's interests lay in that direction anyway. In fact, Wadia Movietone had decided at the end of the 1930s to produce at least one social drama annually alongside the stunt films. Thus, *Kahan Hai Manzil Teri/ Where Lies Your Destiny* was eventually conceived, with J.B.H. Wadia directing. Contrary to his habitual ways, Patel approved of the film in advance in *Filmindia*,

November 1936: 'In any case, there won't be any Punjab Ka Betas or Rolls Royce Ki Betis in it. Which, you will agree, is all to the good. I am inclined to enthusiastically welcome this reorientation of Wadia's policy. Between you and me, their stunt pictures notwithstanding, I have always had a sneaking admiration for the enterprise and vitality of these Wadia brothers. Being shrewd businessmen they stuck to stunt films so far but now they are beginning to produce a better class of pictures for a more sophisticated class of audience. I hope they will achieve the same success as they have had in their earlier enterprises!' Yet, this undoubtedly well-intentioned critic's wish ignored the different interests at Wadia Movietone.

Nadia and Homi Wadia were in no hurry for any fundamental change in studio profile; quite the contrary. As actress and director they were after all the uncrowned queen and king of the Indian stunt genre, and simultaneously their work was the basic prerequisite for retaining the state of limbo in their private life.

They found a romantic temporary solution. Homi Wadia bought a small beach house made of bamboo at Juhu beach, half-an-hour's drive from the edge of town. Beneath the palm trees there, the two of them set up a home far from home to which they could withdraw whenever they felt like it. Behind the open kitchen and living room, the covered veranda opened to a fantastic view out to sea. In this tropical idyll, Homi and Nadia exchanged garlands of flowers—an Indian engagement, an oath of faithfulness, a readiness to wait. For the time being, everything could stay as it was for Homi and Nadia, even though others were striving for change with all their power.

A Tradition of Entertainment

It does not take a lot of imagination to visualize moments in Nadia's life when she felt sick and tired of the exclusiveness of the Parsi community. At the same time the idea seems absurd as, through her films, she had herself become part of the community. The Wadia brothers, and Nadia through association, were heirs to a very specific Parsi tradition of entertainment and, in the final analysis, their films must be seen in the light of this particular tradition. Parsi–Gujarati theatre is seen as the direct precursor of Indian cinema. It was a colourful mixture of urban entertainment that developed in the middle of the nineteenth century in reaction to a particular form of British flaccidity. At the end of the eighteenth century, the colonial power had built theatres in India in which groups of English amateur actors provided light entertainment for their own people. This trend lasted until about 1830, after which the amateur performers held no fascination for anyone any more. The British theatre culture in India decayed, as did the buildings. To start with, no one really knew what to do with the unintentional legacy, and the houses were auctioned. One of the buyers was a Parsi merchant by the name of Sir Jamsetjee Jeejeebhoy, and the contract was signed by his friend Bomanjee Hormusji, a theatre enthusiast and member of the Wadia family. Around Jamsetjee Jeebeebhoy, a new Parsi theatre scene was established. Like at Wadia Movietone decades later, it was the cosmopolitan openness of the Parsis, a shared humour and pioneering spirit that provided the foundation for this new branch of entertainment.

A musty ghost pervaded the stages taken over from the British—an old-fashioned air which had limited popular appeal. But Jamsetjee Jeejeebhoy had discovered his metier and was on the lookout for a new performance location. A rich Parsi businessman eventually provided a plot in Grant Street, one of the main streets in the legendary Bombay workers' quarters of Black Town. Moving to this area, carefully avoided by Europeans, proved a stroke of good fortune. With the opening of the Grant Road Theatre, Jamsetjee Jeejeebhoy conquered a new audience whose preferences were to fundamentally influence the development of Parsi theatre: a commercially successful light theatre, mixing elements of various influences.

The Parsi pioneers of entertainment took over the proscenium stage from the British, which, with its curtain and intricately painted sets, was hitherto unknown to Indian audiences. The most modern stage technology was imported from England. And where content was concerned, Jamsetjee Jeejeebhoy was guided initially by the light comedies and farces that the British had previously taken to the stage. However, performances were no longer in English, but in Indian languages. Most importantly, he lowered the price of tickets, and thus Parsi theatre became entertainment within everyone's reach. The audience was grateful to him, and came to his performances in swarms. The amateur performers soon became professional, and in other parts of Bombay and other cities, ensemble theatres were founded. The programme was made to suit the audience's taste above all else. As there was no obligation to provide a clear moral in performances, European and Indian traditions and elements of style were mixed cheerfully and easily. Much of this can be found in Nadia films, as well, not least the sheer desire for cultural amalgamation.

The supreme decree of the Parsi theatre was its popular appeal. The language spoken on the stage and the stories were comprehensible and didn't require any previous knowledge or education. This was also a basic premise for J.B.H. Wadia with his screenplays. Just as in Parsi theatre plays, the Nadia films were also bound to a certain realism that lead to identification for the audience. The subjects had traits borrowed as generously from the European history of theatre as from Indian folklore and mythology. The cultural origin was not important—the main thing was that the themes were received favourably by the audience. Popular, for example, were stories of mix-ups and plays about uncertain identity, also a leitmotif of many Nadia films. In *Hurricane Hansa*, Nadia plays a Hindu child brought up by a Muslim family; in *Hunterwali*, she is a princess and at the same time, hidden behind a mask, the avenger of the poor; in *Baghdad Ka Jadoo* (1956), she plays the daughter of a minister of a state who was kidnapped as a baby by gypsies and grows up a gypsy girl. A sub-genre of these stories of mix-ups, the cross-dressing comedies popular in Parsi theatre, was part of Nadia's screen repertoire. While in the Indian stage tradition this was restricted to men playing female roles—the popular roly-poly Bal Gandharva was engaged just for this—when Nadia disguised herself as a man and could be seen as a frequenter of bars in *Muqabala* or as 'Prince of the Seas' in *Bagdhad Ka Jadoo*, she was entering new territory. And yet that was accepted by her audience with scarcely the batting of an eyelid. These carnival-like escapades wouldn't have been tolerated as easily had it not been for the theatre tradition.

As schoolchildren, the Wadia brothers often went to the Parsi theatre with their parents, and at an early age they developed a feeling for the preferences of the audience. The spectacular stage effects in which the Parsi theatre had specialized were guaranteed to drive the audience into raptures. What went down particularly well with the viewers were the marvels of Indian mythology, presented for the first time on stage. Headlines were created, for example, by a sword fight with flying sparks, in which the actors were dangerously wired up and connected beneath their costumes. Everything that exploded, thundered, flew through the air on stage was greeted with great applause—and was to be found later in the Wadia films. The drama of the Nadia films, too, the numerous saved-in-the-nick-of-time stories, the cliffhangers and the chronological narration are no less a legacy of this theatre culture.

The Clacking of Indian Castanets in Baghdad

Nadia's dancing talents—in as far as they were supposed to be originally Indian—seemed rather laughable and didn't fit at all to her physiognomy. There were two possible ways of dealing with this handicap. When the story in a particular film—like *Hunterwali* or *Tigress* for example—didn't allow otherwise, a supporting actress, or the rival, had to take over the singing and dancing, so as not to disappoint the audience. In this manner, Nadia's dancing talent remained invisible and dormant. Nadia had, however, developed considerable choreographic ability, ranging from Greek-inspired expression dance to American tap dancing, during her time as a dancer on tour with Madame Astrova. The Wadia brothers endeavoured to find opportunities to put Nadia's abilities in the spotlight. Some stories seem to have been constructed so as to allow Nadia to show what she could do. The results are definitely original.

In *Bambaiwali* (1941), Nadia plays the director of a modern ladies' sports school. An illustration of her teaching in the film is a self-choreographed dance with clubs. As a teacher she is a kind of singing cheerleader in a trouser suit who comes whizzing down a chute into the scene. In each hand she swings a club alight at both ends, twirling them artistically. The pupils, uniformly dressed in a sailor style, follow her rhythm. It is a mixture of cabaret, song, southern European folk dance and athletic gymnastic exercises that ends with prima donna Nadia doing the splits. In *Muqabala*, she incorporates her fencing and tap-dancing talents in the role of the spoilt twin sister. Particularly fetching are her dance numbers in *Bagdhad Ka Jadoo*, where she shows her Arabian fans that blondes too can do the belly dance. The film, an adaptation of the *One Thousand and One Night* tales which were popular in India, tells the story of the feisty stepdaughter of a gypsy king and her ascension to queen of the gypsies in Baghdad after surmounting countless difficulties. Although not a gypsy by birth, this honour is bestowed upon her. As proof of the successful assimilation, the viewer watches Nadia perform fiery gypsy dances. In figure-accentuating flouncy and frilly clothes, she dances an Indian–Spanish fantastical dance with a 'real' gypsy woman, during which imaginary castanets clack in the air, and hips, arms and legs rotate almost quicker than the eye can follow. This truly multicultural performance is made complete acoustically with a Jacques–Offenbach–Mozart melody rendered suitably Indian.

A Helpful Network

In order to promote the colourful boulevard entertainment, the Parsi theatre used publicity strategies that were new at the time. From posters to brightly printed tickets and fliers, they pulled out all the stops. In spite of this, the well-oiled machinery collapsed when the first talkies came to the Indian screen. Up against this competition, stage entertainment stood little chance. Instead of mourning for what had been, lots of people in Parsi theatre decided to join the film industry. For years they dominated the film business in Bombay and Calcutta. They had the lion's share of the film theatres and distribution firms, and the Wadias weren't the only Parsi producers.

For JBH and Homi, small advantages in being Parsis began in childhood through acquaintanceship with a Parsi cinema owner, who let his little Parsi friends creep secretly into the film theatre. Later, when the brothers required permission to film in difficult locations such as railway bridges, it was always much easier to achieve their goal if the stationmaster was a Parsi. They didn't need to know one another personally; there existed an almost incredible fundamental solidarity that could be relied upon. In one typical example, JBH tells how the Parsi owner of the Super Cinema went about promoting one of his early films. He placed himself at the doorway to the cinema in person, and fervently praised the new climaxes and the unusual nature of the film to families walking by. An admittedly laborious form of propaganda, it was said to be effective nonetheless: Bombay is still famous for the speed at which word of mouth spreads.

Cover of programme booklet, Jungle Princess

Cover of programme booklet, Circus Queen

The Wadia brothers themselves were always ready to experiment with publicity. Alongside the usual advertisements and posters, Wadia Movietone started trailers—earlier than other Indian studios—in which a few stunts were shown and the stars introduced along with the adventures that awaited them. Although every new Nadia film had a self-contained plot that was in no way linked to the previous and the subsequent production, the films were always announced as 'Diamond Thriller Number xy'. The idea of a series was emphasized based on a concept effective on an audience not far removed to that of soaps today: a viewer could be sure of seeing a crowd of familiar faces playing the clown, or villains, beside Nadia in the main role in a 'Diamond Thriller'. This continuity was welcomed by the audience and certainly played a significant role in the loyalty of many fans.

Wadia Movietone also paid great attention to the programme booklets as part of the promotion strategy. For many Nadia films, these are all that have survived. The table of contents, differing widely in composition, is therefore all the more appreciated. In the programme booklet to the now vanished *Lutaru Lalna*, for example, Nadia addresses her audience as 'I, Indira, the almighty princess of the country of Ramnagar!' and announces what adventures are in store for her, who her enemies and who her friends are. 'Among other things I'll save the orphan child Vimla from the clutches of Durjan. On the back of my horse Punjab Ka Beta we'll cross the colossal canyons on loose planks that serve as our bridges ...' Back then it was the lovingly designed covers, though, that rendered the programme booklets desirable collector's items—they were colourfully made collages, with Nadia in the centre, usually in an action shot. All around this were a plethora of comic-like sketches of the anticipated attractions. On the cover of the *Circus Queen* booklet, for example, you see Nadia in a Russian–Bavarian folk costume, wielding a whip, her fingernails long and painted red. Apart from this, the collage shows in a clockwise direction: Nadia in a cage as a lion-tamer; trapeze artistes and a high-wire walker; John Cawas engaged in a fight; a procession of a decorated elephant herd; a party trick by clever dog Moti; an oriental dancer couple entwined acrobatically; and a circus tent, visitors going in. These scenes and a film announcement in three languages fit into the format of a large chocolate bar.

6

THE WILD DAYS

Punjab Mail, 1939

With the outbreak of the Second World War, the conflicts between the Indian independence movement and the British colonial power grew more acute. The overtly racist policy of aggression on the part of the Europeans made itself felt in the cinema too. With a focussed gaze, the censors searched Indian films for latent criticism or anti-colonial propaganda against England. That they found nothing to quibble about in the current Nadia films, *Punjab Mail* (1939), *Lutaru Lalna* (1939) and *Diamond Queen* (1940), is astounding. A possible explanation may be found in the numerous films about India produced in the West at that time. Films like *The Tiger of Eschnapur* (Richard Eichberg, Germany, 1937) or *The Drum* (Alexander Korda, GB, 1938) were so obviously propagandistic that the responsible censors were completely numbed to a more subtle film language.

One report in a German newspaper about the filming of *The Tiger of Eschnapur* wrote: 'It was incredibly difficult to get along with the people there. They worked as slow as snails and some natives were so stupid that it would have been easier to use dogs.' Richard Eichberg made the film based on Thea von Harbour's novel which was again adapted for the screen by Fritz Lang in 1959. *The Tiger of Eschnapur* is about a Parisian dancer who is kidnapped and brought to India by an Indian maharaja in love with her. She is at last freed from this terrible, torturous imprisonment by her faithful French lover. The film is based on fact, the prologue claims. This spicy piece of information certainly helped the pseudo-exotic drama to decisively influence the German picture of India. When the film came to the Indian cinemas two years later, it caused an uproar all over the country. There was considerable disgust at the ingratitude of the German 'Tobis Film Expedition', as can be read in the editorial of *Filmindia* in September 1937. The vilification in the German press, with their detailed horror stories about the inefficiency of the extras, thoroughly discredited the widespread assistance the unit received, in particular from the maharaja of Udaipur who had generously put his palace, his soldiers, his servants and his elephants at the disposal of the filming crew. And then the film itself was far from charitable in its depiction of Indians. The maharaja in the film is an unpredictable madman whose life revolves solely around the sating of his ravenous sexual appetite. The white dancer from Paris is abandoned to his desires, utterly helpless in his harem.

The Tiger of Eschnapur is a typical example of the way in which many film production companies in the West used India as a backdrop. From the days of the silent movies, the exotic projection of the Orient as a place of unimaginable luxury with unbridled sexuality and opaque customs was quite popular. As compared to earlier films such as Theda Bara's *Salomé* (1918) or *The Victoria Cross* (1917), the films of the 1930s and 1940s were characterized by an open racism—with films like *Lives of a Bengal Lancer* (Henry Hathaway, USA, 1935), *Wee Willie Winkie* (John Ford, USA, 1937) or *The Drum* being prime examples. The aggressive slandering of Indians in German, British and American productions was consciously regarded in India as a strategy of retaining colonial power. As, for example, Khwaja Ahmad Abbas writes about the Hollywood film *Gunga Din*: 'It is an Imperialist propaganda of the crudest, the most vulgar sort and depicts Indians as nothing better than sadistic barbarians. It will make the stomachs of every Indian—and every fair-minded foreigner—turn with disgust.

Some of the scenes in it are revolting, nauseating.' Among the stereotypes in these films are the naïve native who is either dangerous or stupid, as well as the uncontrollable sexual drive of Indians—the leitmotif of *The Tiger of Eschnapur* as well. *Filmindia* writes about it: 'There are obvious references to the primitive and animal instincts prevalent among the men and the women of India and a laboured attempt has been made to reveal the supposed superiority of the Europeans. *Tiger of Eschnapur* is in short an obnoxious film which is at present doing dirty work in the European countries by defaming Indians and exposing them to the ridicule of the world.' It was no longer enough, it continues, to simply make sure such films are forbidden in India. In helpless anger the text finishes with the question typed in bold: 'What in the world can we do to fight this?'

That Wadia Movietone had more than one answer to this up its sleeve actually surprised only the intellectuals who had long since prided themselves on having never seen a Nadia film. This changed when *Diamond Queen* came to the Indian screens in August 1940. It was a Nadia film with a relatively high budget and the camerawork by R.P. Master, who had just returned from Hollywood, was acclaimed as the most skilful of the year. For Baburao Patel, who admitted in his review in *Filmindia* that he had never yet seen an Indian stunt film, *Diamond Queen* was a real 'a-ha' experience: 'As I was watching the film I was overcome by the suspicion that there was an underlying matter of importance in the wild tumult of fights and stunts. And the producer himself explained to me it was madness with method. The story takes place in "Diamond Town", the studio backdrop for the methodical chaos, and that's where the demand for a better government with just rulers arises. This cinematic plea for a healthy and socially responsible life is presented, however, with such a lightness of touch that one feels optimally entertained and hardly realises that a lesson is being preached.' It had clicked at last!

Tigress in the Struggle for Freedom

For the Wadias, referring to current political themes had been an indispensable element of the Nadia films ever since *Hunterwali*. In an interview in the mid-1980s, J.B.H. Wadia went as far as to say that this was where the actual secret of Nadia's success was to be found: 'In almost every stunt film a social problem was the starting point of the story. Among the themes dealt with were, for example, Hindu–Muslim unity, the emancipation of women, literacy campaigns, the struggle for independence, corruption and land ownership, the black market and so on. Alongside the high technical standard it was this content that made our productions stand out from other stunt films. That's why Nadia films are still remembered today.' Yet the Wadias had good reason for not making a hue and cry about their political ambitions.

The 1930s and 1940s saw the struggle for India's independence gain momentum. At the forefront of the freedom movement was Mahatma Gandhi whose charisma, ascetic lifestyle, but above all the principles of non-violence, passive resistance and non-cooperation with the British colonial government that he expounded found masses upon masses of admirers and adherers. The more desperately the British defended their position as colonial masters through repression, intimidation and naked violence, the more virulent grew the Indians' readiness to organize themselves into resistance. The British increasingly resorted to police-state methods to stamp out the uprisings.

From the mid-1930s, the colonial power altered its strategy with the passing of the Government of India Act, 1935. This reform allowed elected Indian representatives a certain measure of political say at a local level. Part of the efforts also included the release of seventeen documentary films which dealt for the most past with the theme of Gandhi's political work. This cautious liberalization was, like the tried and tested 'divide and rule' strategy, an extremely clever move. It led to sustained and long debates within the independence movement on how much one should submit oneself to the stalling tactics of the British. How long would the road to independence take if progress was made only in tiny steps? Didn't one lose sight, through the pseudo-democratic small successes, of the major aim? Jawaharlal Nehru described the Government of India Act as the 'New Charter of Slavery', an assessment shared by the radical left as well as the pacifist wing of the freedom movement. As a reaction to the repressive policy in their own country, but also with a suspicious gaze at the British restraint in the Spanish Civil War, the Indian National Congress warned the colonial rulers in advance in 1936 that India wouldn't support Britain again in an imperial war.

Regardless of the differences in opinion over how one should behave towards the British, the strategists of the freedom movement were at one in their evaluation that there was great need for action at the local level. In the extremely politicized climate of those years, numerous campaigns were carried out at the grass-roots level, ranging from short-term legal help in the struggle against big landowners to long-term measures such as literacy campaigns. The District Congress Committee from Surat explained for example: 'The village inhabitants are continuously squeezed by moneylenders, big landowners and corrupt officials. The best way to establish contact with the masses and to gain respect from the population is to help them in removing these very difficulties.' Jayaprakash Narayan wrote at around the same time: 'A persecuted, suppressed peasantry cannot fulfil its real place in the national revolution. The peasantry needs to be helped to their feet, they need to be made aware of their power and strengths, they need to be organized and welded together. With the strength of the farmers, the strength of the nation will grow.'

These proclamations read like the plot directions for Nadia's film creations. In contrast to the all-India nature of the freedom struggle, Nadia's terrain was the comparatively comprehensible domain of the village. Inspired by real events, the screenwriter J.B.H. Wadia intensified the conflicts with which his heroine got entangled, while developing and suggesting dramatically clever solutions. 'The viewers always had the impression that the Nadia films dealt with precisely the conflicts that most affected them,' says the Indian film historian P.K. Nair. 'In Nadia, a person had emerged who removed many of the oppressive problems from the world—even if only on-screen. Due to the repressive mood in the country it was often not possible for the farmers and workers to become activists themselves in public—you could be thrown in prison for any little thing. Nadia entered the arena on behalf of these masses, an outsider who came out of nothingness and stood up for the issues of the peasants, of those deprived of their rights and fought at their side. Almost effortlessly, she eliminated collaborators and corrupt big landowners, precisely the people her viewers would also have liked to remove from the world. Naturally, everyone fell in love with Nadia.'

With a stroke of genius, the Wadias' gamble paid off: the daughter of a British soldier had turned into the cult cinematic symbol of the Indian freedom struggle. Nadia personified the constructive counter-image to the demeaning portrait of the supposedly weak, stupid, sex-obsessed Indian in the films of the imperialistic West. She was a popular figure, as unique and radical as the conditions that produced her, with whom the masses identified. Homi Wadia admits that they had certainly been a little uneasy about this, and always took appropriate care that the screenplay provided pro-Indian patriotic statements for Nadia which were integrated into the individual stories.

In *Bambaiwali*, a freedom dance was performed with this aim in mind, the message of which is clear from the backdrop. Nadia dances with some schoolgirls in the silhouette-like outline of the map of India in which little stage windows are stamped out for each dancer as in an Advent calendar. In *Tigress* (1947), Nadia holds aloft a clump of native soil and delivers a fiery plea citing large-scale landholding as the root of all evil for the peasantry—but words alone don't have the desired success. As a teacher, she plays the saviour of a poor widow forced by villains to sell her modest piece of land. In her fight against the feudal lords who know every trick in the book, Nadia has to draw on all her skills. In one of the many incidents, she escapes arrest for her inflammatory speech. In another, she rescues the cheated widow from a burning house. So as not to be recognized on her courageous sorties against the corrupt state, Nadia appears in a comical, yet erotic tiger costume that suits her very well, in particular the mask with its little ears. In close combat, she makes frequent use of her claws, and hisses fearlessly at her adversaries. With all this strenuous activity, leading to the obligatory downfall of the greed-driven collaborators, Nadia the teacher doesn't get round to much teaching, but her fans are ready to forgive her for this. In the wild days of the independence movement, life on the street was certainly more important than what was taught in the colonial educational institutions.

Still from Tigress

Tigress shows how Nadia used her sexuality on-screen as a liberating weapon. The colonial regime had perfected a system of suppression over a century that also made use of psychological mechanisms. In colonial ideology, Indian men were regarded simultaneously as being bestially sex-obsessed and weak and feminine. In contrast to this was the European man's self-image as a strong, courageous bringer of civilization, who remains in control of his drives and physical strength even in extreme situations. Contemporary English novels and films propagated and cemented these colonial clichés more brazenly than ever before in Nadia's time.

Thus, it is all the more remarkable that Nadia moved outside this framework in her films. While as a white European she represented something of a cinematic arrowhead of the freedom struggle for her fans, as a fictional character she synthesized a powerful alternative to the well-known gender roles. Behind her feminine, European exterior were hidden qualities, considered as male since times immemorial, that she deftly employed for the goals of the freedom struggle: courage, strength, fighting spirit, determination. This fictive combination of traditionally feminine and masculine forms of behaviour functioned like an allegory of the strategy with which the militarily inferior Indians attempted to conquer the armed colonial lords. Certainly, the willingness of the Indian public to accept the white Nadia as their heroine must also be regarded as evidence of the highly developed culture of tolerance in this state of many peoples. As though it were something quite banal, one Nadia fan said: 'She spoke Hindi and occasionally wore a sari—that in itself made her Indian enough for us.'

In the Censor-free Film Village

Nothing could be more wrong than to reduce the Nadia films to the level of simple political agitation through hermeneutic tricks. The Indian public was downright allergic to this kind of educational sermonizing. In contrast to many other countries, almost all attempts in India to influence the masses through film in one or another political direction resulted in flops. The Wadias were well aware that their audience was not looking for lectures, even if these would have reflected their interests. Nonetheless, J.B.H. Wadia would have yielded to the temptation perhaps of using his films even more explicitly for political interest. He had been involved in the struggle for India's independence for years both as a member of the Congress Party and as an intellectual with a developed social conscience. When he was elected chairman of the Film Advisory Board, he took up office without the slightest hesitation. This body, initiated by the British, decided which foreign films would be shown in the Indian cinemas and aimed, with the introduction of newsreels, to keep the public up-to-date with political happenings. Always on the lookout for new areas of activity, JBH was one of the first Indian producers to work on these news programmes. These short documentary films were not without their share of controversy due to the conditions of censorship. In the field of feature films, censorship was less problematic. Perhaps in the case of the Nadia films, the censorship guidelines presented only an apparent obstacle, a constructive limitation, the scaling of which, as so often the case in film history, simply called for and enhanced the creative insights of the film-makers.

In questions of censorship, the British apparently felt committed to their image as the oldest democracy of the world, even in India. The authorities allowed basically everything to be shown on-screen apart from direct criticism of the British presence or undisguised propagation of Indian independence. These regulations were indeed much more liberal than those that came into place after independence. As long as film producers transported contemporary themes into allegorical, fairy-tale or fantastical planes they were left pretty much to their own devices in the creation of their films. Producers, however, often found ways to beat the rules and incorporate subtle nationalist messages. And the public immediately caught on to these subterfuges as was witnessed in the spontaneous reaction to the slightest political reference. Even in shallow mythological productions, with no narrative connection, if a small portrait of Gandhi was sighted hanging on a wall of the living room, enthusiastic applause broke out. More subtle intimations were also recognized with exactitude. In *Hunterwali Ki Beti*, there is a dubious minor figure who wears a pith helmet. With this symbol of British colonial presence on his head he is barked at wildly by a dog and pursued. He complains angrily to the dog owner, who only says: 'If you remove your hat, the dog will immediately calm down!' and this promptly happens.

Most of the Nadia stories play in a curious timeless realm where kings, ministers and civil servants rule over a village-like community. The people are a diverse mixture of peasants, workers, children, rogues and housewives. It is a fantasy community in a fantasy time that doesn't feel bound to reality in the slightest. Yet, the characters—as well as the studio settings—represent something of the essence of an Indian village, an effect that is further intensified by the strong true-to-type performances of Nadia and her colleagues. At first glance, many of the figures can be categorized as rich, poor, vulnerable, shady villains or funny jesters. The village community made up of the Wadia ensemble provided a 'home-base' of solidarity for Nadia in her films, serving as a studio home and the point from which she takes off on her hot pursuit outdoors. Conflicts in the village were usually brewing from the word go and public spaces—half-open halls, unwalled courtyards, covered assembly podiums—were preferred so that at the moment of escalation it just so happens that the entire group of inhabitants are gathered together. While the films seldom—and only briefly—play in poor houses, numerous fights may take place in the generous chambers of kings' palaces or the luxurious offices of a businessman, ravaged with merry regularity. For all the fairy-tale elements, though, the furnishings don't seem historic. On the contrary, kings are driven in cars to their palaces where telephones are as natural a part of the interior as Western sofa sets.

Thanks to this spatial shift to seemingly naïve fantasy worlds, the Wadia brothers usually had nothing to fear from the censorship authorities. The positive, and definitely calculated, side effect of the fairy-tale narrative style was a universal comprehensibility. Not only the Indian public, but viewers in other colonies too could see their lives reflected in the individual stories—albeit reduced to simple structures, clear power machinations and typecast characters. The village ambience of the majority of the Nadia films was, moreover, a milieu that evoked a pleasant, familiar feeling of home amongst the urban public. Most of the workers—who formed the core of Nadia's fan following—had moved as emigrants to the cities not long before and often found it difficult to fit in with the more complicated, urban lifestyle. The village location also made it effortlessly possible to simplify political conflicts. The Wadias always limited themselves in the Nadia films to one central problem that, taken out of the confusing complexity of the political reality, lost its alarming aspect. This approach led to the Nadia films becoming a kind of subtle propaganda to enlighten the people.

DIAMOND QUEEN

Diamond Queen was their showcase for this process.

The film takes place in 'Diamond Town', a little town that owes its existence to a diamond mine. It is an idyllic little spot and Nadia's home town to which she is returning after completing her education in Bombay. In the meantime, however, the mine has also enticed villains who are stirring up the peaceful village community. They appear for the first time when respectable citizens are announcing a literacy campaign in the Diamond Hotel: 'We want to finally cast off the shackles of slavery! Our campaign is the first and the most important step for freedom. How can a nation liberate itself when only eight per cent of the population can read and write? We want to make the light of knowledge shine brightly in Diamond Town!' The activists don't get any further; the speech is drowned out by wild demands for music and dancing. The hotel owner submits meekly to the loutish villains and sends his own daughter to the dance floor. This is Nadia's first encounter with the new inhabitants of Diamond Town as she happens to be cycling past. She makes short shrift of throwing the grumbling drinkers out of the hotel, with a handsome, powerful man coming to her assistance. This is Diler (John Cawas) who plays a very interesting role in this film. The older inhabitants haven't a good word to say about him, he is a thief, and indeed after the fighting he disappears as quickly as he

Poster of Diamond Queen

appeared—on Nadia's bicycle. Nadia instinctively recognizes, however, that the dashing rebel is on the right side.

Nadia's active support of the literacy campaign is only one course of the meal offered by the film, the staking of a political position. In real life, the Indian independence movement faced similar difficulties to those of activists in Diamond Hotel. These were the consequences of the outbreak of war in Europe: two days after the invasion of Poland by the German Wehrmacht, the British Viceroy Lord Linlithgow had declared that India was now at war against the fascist states. Deeply angered that the British had delivered a declaration of war for India without consulting the Congress or other Indian representatives, the Congress Working Committee passed a resolution. As long as the British didn't openly state in unmistakable terms its aims of war, also in regard to India's future, Indians would refuse to fight fascism on behalf of the British. Nehru and other socialist leaders of the independence movement distrusted the British interpretation of democracy that limited a people's right to self-determination to Europe. He said India could not participate in a war that was conducted in the defence of freedom and democracy while this very freedom was being denied to India. A free, democratic India would proudly stand beside other free nations in mutual defence.

In spite of the boycott, the war had induced a sudden upheaval of the Indian economy. While both the weapons and exports industries boomed, enormous bottlenecks were experienced in providing for the population, just as during the First World War. These were ideal conditions for the emergence of a black market—and all that comes with it. This was the tricky subject matter of *Diamond Queen*. Since the outbreak of war, heavy industries—including the diamond business which was important for arms—had achieved a strategic importance worldwide, and dubious figures like the new inhabitants of Diamond Town had come into money and power in many parts of India. The villains in Diamond Hotel, the film narrates, work hand in hand with the new maharaja. This is a man with no conscience as revealed by both his clothes and the brutality he wants to unleash on Nadia. 'This woman is dangerous for us. We must act before she can spread her ideas!' he explains to his rogues-in-arms. Nadia is to be killed. The villains follow Nadia as she rides on horseback to a romantic rendezvous by the waterfall. It's there that the dramatic stunt sequences ensue in which a small village boy had a mortal accident.

The pursuit reveals more than just the true colours of the new men of Diamond Town. Together with Nadia, the public discovers that her suitor, Diler, is fighting the corrupt villains in the manner of Robin Hood. His father, who discovered the mine and is therefore its rightful owner, had been murdered by the diamond poachers and as he lay dying he asked his son to avenge this injustice. However, his existence beyond the fringes of society in Diamond Town isn't particularly glorious. In contrast to Nadia who is loved and admired by the population for her Robin Hood act in *Hunterwali*, John Cawas encounters distrust and contempt in spite of all his good intentions, right up to the end of the film. Nadia can, however, understand Diler using illegal methods in his quest to regain his rightful fortune bit by bit. But her vision goes further: Nadia wants peace and justice to reign supreme in Diamond Town again. That's why in a letter to the prince of the land she reports the unbearable situation, the capricious ruler, and the need and fear of the people. She makes a plea to Prince Ranjit to personally ensure justice in Diamond Town and restore order. He agrees, and appears in disguise far earlier than expected. As a bizarre town-dweller who claims to be a friend of the prince, he listens to the complaints of the people. Diler uses the day of the official visit to surrender to the authorities. Nadia has urged him to give up his 'criminal' existence so that she may marry him some day. In the presence of the prince, a court case unravels in which Diler is reinstated and the band of villains sentenced. The corrupt maharaja tries to escape but Nadia doesn't allow him to get away. She clings to the back of the retreating carriage, the soles of her shoes sending up sparks, and manages to recapture the head of the villainous gang. With this final stunt, she becomes the 'Diamond Queen' of Diamond Town.

THE CINEMA FOLLOWERS OF ROY

Nadia's determined aversion to taking the law into one's own hands in *Diamond Queen* is connected to J.H.B. Wadia's activities outside the studio. The beginning of the Second World War saw the end of the screenwriter's career as a producer. He actively entered politics at the side of M.N. Roy.

JBH had followed the life of M.N. Roy with the greatest of interest. As the son of a simple teacher, M.N. Roy had fought in a revolutionary guerrilla organization in his youth for the liberation of Bengal and became famous in the 1920s when, together with Lenin, he wrote the tenets of the Comintern on decolonization. There followed long sojourns in Mexico, China and in Tashkent where he co-founded the Communist Party. The fervent communist also visited Berlin where he met Marlene Dietrich and Ellen, his future wife and closest colleague. During the Stalin era, Roy did turn away from Moscow, returning to India where he was promptly arrested and spent the next six years of his life in prison, a period that he used predominantly for reading and thinking. Like JBH, M. N. Roy felt a close bond to the policy of the Indian National Congress—until the war began.

JBH had got to know M.N. Roy by chance. Wadia Movietone regularly inserted advertisements for Nadia films in various newspapers, including Roy's newspaper *Independent India Weekly.* And thus, one day, a friend of the politician's came knocking at the office to request a little support for Roy's stay in Bombay. Instead of alms, JBH and Hilla Wadia generously offered their villa as accommodation. That the secret service would look askance at this form of hospitality didn't worry them a whit. The house guest became the closest of friends. JBH admired the self-taught M.N. Roy for his extensive knowledge, his cosmopolitan world view, his tireless involvement for democracy and humanism. In Roy, he had found a friend, a kindred spirit, as well as a mentor. In the 1980s, J.B.H. Wadia wrote a very personalized biography about the man in which he describes M.N. Roy as 'the intellectual conscience of India'. The Bengali who achieved the status of guru was, as JBH emphasizes, in every sense also a mondaine hedonist:

> Many meetings [of the Royists] were also held at the Casa [da Vinci] and many memorable decisions were taken there. Drinks, of course, preceded dinner and were followed by appetisers at dinner table and wines and liqueurs. Had an honest Congressman been a witness to our revelry, he would have been shocked at the 'orgy'. The parties generally lasted till the witching hours of the night and sometimes even into the small hours of the morning.[9]

[9] Wadia, J.B.H., *M.N. Roy: The Man*, New Delhi: Popular Prakashan, 1987.

When the German Wehrmacht marched into Paris in the summer of 1940, the Royists separated from the Indian National Congress and formed the Radical Democratic Party of India. The time had come for M.N. Roy, J.B.H. Wadia and their party friends to join the ranks of the anti-fascist alliance in order to stop the further advance of the National Socialists and the Japanese. 'India's freedom was, for better or for worse, connected to the freedom of the world,' Wadia writes. 'A fascist victory would have turned back the clock of history. India's chances of self-liberation would have been lost in a fascist victory, buried beneath the rebirth of the Middle Ages.' The Royists observed with concern as many Indian nationalists, following the simple dictum 'The enemy of my enemy is my friend', celebrated every victory of Hitler as a nail in the coffin of British imperialism. Hitler, who had spoken benevolently of the 'Indian Aryan' in *Mein Kampf*, and had taken a reversed Hindu swastika as his party's symbol, was perceived as a real danger by just a small number of Indian activists until the attack on the Soviet Union in 1942. Roy and the Radical Democratic Party crusaded against this 'bankrupt explanation' and 'philosophical immaturity'. In doing so, they adopted an outsider's position and, as supposed British sympathizers, made many enemies in their own country.

Almost simultaneously with the founding of the Radical Democratic Party in 1940, *Diamond Queen* came out of the Wadia studios. It had as little in common with classical agitation films as *Miss Frontier Mail*, *Hurricane Hansa* or *Lutaru Lalna* did, and yet one sensed between the images a different, more openly political position in regard to what was going on in the real world. Though in full possession of her fighting skills in *Diamond Queen*, Nadia makes an exception and hands the role of the good outlaw to the male lead, John Cawas, while she plays an educated outsider influenced by the West who only fights when she is left with no other choice. As a courageous harbinger of civilization, she is determined to remove the ruling, thieving law of the strong in Diamond Town in favour of a modern community of solidarity. Her tactics are clear in the loving admonishment to her father when she explains he shouldn't take it for granted that he can open her letters any more: 'In Bombay this would be considered bad manners!' *Diamond Queen* differs from Nadia's other films above all through Nadia's acceptance of the precedence of state authorities.

In the film, Nadia asks Prince Ranjit for his help which finally leads to a fair court case and the reinstatement of the lost order. This ending is easily recognizable as a plea from the lawyer J.B.H. Wadia for democratic jurisdiction. At a time when military alternatives to democracy were becoming popular once more, resolving the story in this way implied an unambiguous political statement. Yet JBH made sure *Diamond Queen* couldn't possibly be regarded as a pro-British statement. The visit of Prince Ranjit to Diamond Town had much more in common with a very old Indian tradition. Before an Indian prince could ascend the throne, he was duty bound to travel through his lands disguised as a simple man to get to know the living conditions of his people first-hand. Prince Ranjit's appearance in Diamond Town is reminiscent of this: with an almost sociological interest he mingles with the inhabitants and learns everything he needs to know to be able to conduct a fair hearing at the end. However, this is only possible thanks to Nadia's clever and determined groundwork—an achievement that perfectly matched the aims of the Radical Democratic Party. Nadia's role in *Diamond Queen* was the clearest political partisanship that J.B.H. Wadia as a screenwriter ever asked of the star of his films.

Determined Amusement Despite Power Cuts

'During the Second World War, our troops watched loads of Hindi films in itinerant sixteen-millimetre screenings. The Nadia films were among the most popular,' recalls J.B.H. Wadia, not without pride. 'Suddenly, however, some high-ranking officers discovered the revolutionary nature of the films and feared the disturbing effect they might have on the soldiers' morale. Behind a facade of stunts and action, the slogan "liberation from tyranny" could, after all, always be heard. This small group of incensed military men from Sind believed they had stumbled upon a subtle attack on British imperialism. As a consequence, our films were brought to the attention of the censorship authorities in Bombay once again. But they detected nothing subversive in my stories. The loudly proclaimed reproaches ebbed away to a soft whimper. And so the Wadia ship was able to cheerfully continue on its voyage on the great ocean of entertainment.'

This voyage made swift progress: the war in far-off Europe proved extremely energizing for the film business across the length and breadth of the country. For one thing, Indians had more money again and they spent no small portion of it on entertainment, with cinema dominating what was available. Another aspect was that the film business provided an excellent place for the laundering of money generated in the black market. Studios sprung up like mushrooms—in spite of the war-induced shortage of chemicals and film material. Until 1939, Indian studios had been supplied almost exclusively by German firms. The bottleneck resulting from the war was ironed out by a law described by film historians, in retrospect, as a blessing. During war time, no film could be longer than 12,000 feet, which corresponds roughly to a two-hour running time. As if by magic, the dry, endless dialogues of Indian social dramas suddenly disappeared. Indian cinema became livelier, pacier, and more action-driven.

Just how far removed the actual war locations were from India until the summer of 1942 is disclosed, for example, by a small caricature in *Filmindia*. It shows the actress Naseem, clad in an elegant sari, turning round in fright at a toy bomb. Beneath it is the caption: 'Naseem would likely faint in fear at the very first bomb!' To most Indians, the war still appeared an exotic adventure. Nobody guessed that soon famine and the dramatic battles in neighbouring Burma would threaten peace in India. Certainly, the frequent power cuts and the flourishing black market made everyday living a trial for many people, yet, as is so often the case in restless times, life also had its charms. In the face of all the adversities, there was a very great need for distraction and entertainment of every form. The ballroom in the Taj Mahal Hotel was often brimming over even when no lantern lit the way outside. When *Diamond Queen* came to the cinemas in August 1940, the technically mature, well-directed stunt film corresponded to the risqué, fast pace of time prevalent in those years. The film was a box office smash, and with it Nadia and Homi Wadia had reached the zenith of their shared success.

7

A FEMINIST ICON

A FEMINIST ICON

Diamond Queen, 1940

For feminists, the discovery of Fearless Nadia is a stroke of luck. The manner in which, from the beginning of her long film career, she fought, more or less explicitly, for the equality of women comes across as very modern and extremely inspiring from today's perspective. Her films, *Bambaiwali* in particular, also serve as a reminder that there has been a women's movement in India, whose effectiveness and determination particularly during the struggle for independence astounds some Western feminists today. An exploration of the blatant or underground connections between Nadia's films and the Indian women's movement reveals that feminism is not an invention of the Western world.

Despite some very obvious changes for the better, women in India are disadvantaged, oppressed and excluded from public life in a variety of ways. From harassment for dowry at home to sexual harassment at the workplace, the lot of a large number of urban Indian women is unenviable. The daily routine for the female inhabitants of slums and villages is even more gloomy: for wretched wages, women carry out the hardest work in the fields, break stones, pour tar, haul cement at road-works or building sites in the searing heat. Hand in hand with this they are expected to complete all the household chores from cooking and fetching water to the raising of children—and on top of it submit themselves wholeheartedly and with love to the man they are assigned to in marriage. The mindset of the society at large harks back to the Middle Ages.

'May you be the mother of a hundred sons', is an old Sanskrit blessing for young brides, clearly defining the role of the grown woman. Daughters, traditionally regarded as a burden for the family, should ideally be transferred as young as possible from the control of their fathers to the keeping of a husband, where they may hope for a little respect as mothers—of sons, naturally. As far back as 2000 years ago, the Indian lawmaker Manu formulated these rules, the consequences of which are being felt to this day:

> ... [a woman] should not have independence. A woman should not try to separate herself from her father, her husband, or her sons ... She should always be cheerful, and clever at household affairs; she should keep her utensils well polished and not have too free a hand in spending. When her father, or her brother with her father's permission, gives her to someone, she should obey that man while he is alive and not violate her vow to him when he is dead.[10]

Over the decades, films have mirrored this anti-feminist viewpoint and have negatively influenced existing gender relations in a society that is largely illiterate. The ideal of the perfect woman is seen in the figure of the mythological goddess Sita. In the Ramayan, Sita speaks the central sentence: 'A woman's god is her husband/He is her friend/He is her guru/Her own life counts for less/Than the happiness of her husband.' Practically every new actress who makes it to the top in Indian cinema appears to fervently emulate this maxim on the big screen. Thus, it is not surprising that many Indian feminists view popular cinema as the worst enemy of the women's movement. Back in the 1950s, there was an initiative by educators and social workers

[10] Doniger, Wendy, trans., *The Laws of Manu*, London, New York: Penguin Books, 1991.

who demanded that the government take action against the reactionary depiction of women in cinema. In the 1970s, a feminist organization in Ahmedabad explored the contemporary image of women in Indian cinema and went on to publish the deeply shocking findings. Numerous films in the period of study revolved around male lead characters to whom young, very beautiful women were simply ornamental accessories. The female characters in the films were on the whole hysteric, submissive and as a rule marriage was their sole aim. When it came to marriage, character didn't play a role; beauty and money alone determined the worth of women in the films. There was a tendency to depict them as utterly stupid which also explained their emotional overreaction as they see-sawed back and forth between convulsive sobbing and intense happiness. Women in films, it seemed, were not capable of either making rational decisions or coming up with sensible utterances; instead, they were very frequently raped, beaten up and imaginatively tortured. Less academic but just as effective as the women's group from Ahmedabad, the women's group 'Pennurimai Iyakkam' from Madras became active at around the same time and was considered militant: for a while they systematically threw cow dung at posters of films which showed women in a poor light!

When the Heroine Was Still Allowed to Work

In the cinematic world of pitiful daughters, devoted wives and self-sacrificing mothers, Fearless Nadia is a truly remarkable figure. But she was in no way a unique case. In her day, the 1930s and 1940s, Indian women were as much in the forefront of the freedom struggle as their male counterparts. In those days, strong individualistic female figures existed in Indian cinema also—unlike in subsequent decades—and pitched themselves against conventions. V. Shantaram, for example, created a feminist milestone with *Kunku* (aka *Duniya Na Maane*) in 1937. It tells the story of the life-loving but orphaned Neera who is forced by her uncle into marriage with a man old enough to be her father. Instead of submitting to her role, Neera rebels against her fate and adopts the role of a wildcat at home and in the neighbourhood, revealing the pseudo-youthful gestures of her husband in public, terrorizing his scheming aunt, beating up the arrogant stepson and having her own uncle admitted to a madhouse. When her stepdaughter, almost the same age, comes to visit she discovers an intellectual sympathizer: 'I want to show the world my fury,' she explains to her. 'I hope that my crusade will send fear deep into the hearts of all old men who dare to marry young girls. If only a few girls can be saved in this way my crusade will have succeeded.' However, Neera has only an ambiguous victory to show at the end of the film: to set her free for a better marriage, the repentant husband commits suicide. But the liberated young woman doesn't appear particularly joyful, weeping at the end of the film as she decorates his photo on the home altar with flowers and incense and regards the uncertain future as a widow. In contrast to Nadia in her films, Neera has to undergo immense suffering in *Kunku* to keep the feminist flag flying.

Nadia's contemporary screen sisters were given much stronger roles than cinema heroines of the following decades. The number of films in which women were central to the plot was notably higher. Alongside Nadia, came a series of female stars who were marketed as crowd-pullers in equal measure and who enticed hordes of fans to cinema. Sabita Devi, for example, was one of the frontrunners in the mid-1930s who caused a furore with *Dr Madhurika*. The adaptation of the novel of the same name by K.M. Munshi revolves around an unhappy married couple. Sabita Devi plays the role of a successful doctor married to a lawyer. In the course of the film, it becomes clear that the root of the unhappiness lies solely in the fact that both husband and wife have careers. Consequently, she resigns. From then on she is always there for her husband, and their happiness is complete. This extremely successful film made the feminist Kamaladevi Chattopadhyaya fizz with anger: 'One would assume that a doctor is capable of dealing with her life and problems in a sober and scientific manner. But Dr Madhurika's behaviour in the film is surprisingly irrational. In fact, no woman with the slightest shred of human understanding would ever behave in such a laughable way.'

Dr Madhurika is typical of the way career women were depicted in Indian cinema of the 1930s. The female lead may work but stops as soon as she marries. A woman who refuses to become a housewife following a film-marriage is placing herself in danger of becoming a prostitute, even if her profession is a highly respected one such as medicine or law. A more recent example of this anti-feminist film tradition is *Itni Si Baat*, a hit in 1981. In this film, the wife wants to be the breadwinner of the family, but her professionally unsuccessful husband won't hear of it: 'Women only go working to have money for powder and lipstick.' The woman chooses not to listen to her husband and the film shows where this leads to: after a dreadful brothel odyssey she returns repentant to the stove.

Popular Indian film even refuses to realistically depict peasant women who, as is well known, do the lion's share of the tilling of the fields in India. If a story takes place in a village setting, women are almost always singing and chatting, sitting at the edge of the field. Sometimes they also dance through paddy fields or nibble on sugar cane. They certainly don't seem to work much. Exceptions to these stereotypical women figures are found in the so-called parallel cinema of the country—films with artistic ambitions which often encounter more viewers abroad than in India. Nadia was indeed privileged to be permitted to act the independent woman, often active in a profession and always independent of men, without having to suffer or be humiliated through this. These liberties in cinema were withheld from her actress colleagues for the most part. Yet, beyond the conservative film world, Indian women caused quite a rumpus during the independence movement. Lots of female activists attempted to use the momentum of the major political upheavals to bring about changes in the position of women. J.B.H. Wadia followed these developments with great interest. It is certainly no coincidence that Fearless Nadia bore certain resemblances to particular heroines of the anti-colonial struggle.

The Avalanche of Women

For Nadia, any withdrawal to private happiness on the screen was as good as impossible. Usually, the films were long over before the viewer could—with plenty of imagination—envisage a liaison with her good-looking co-fighters John Cawas or Boman Shroff. In this, Nadia corresponded to the contemporary ideal of the fighting woman, consorting with the freedom movement rather than with a man. The inventor of this radical form of female independence was Mahatma Gandhi who, more than any other politician before or after him, concerned himself with the rights of women in India. Gandhi succeeded in initiating hordes of women into the independence movement by calling on them to no longer allow themselves to be abused as 'dolls and objects of lust' but to become instead 'comrades in the service of the community'. Countless women followed his call and, for the first time in the history of the country, participated in political life. Nadia transports the Mahatma's lesson into a formulation of exemplary simplicity in *Diamond Queen*: after a villain has tried to remove her from the picture, she announces, 'Indian women are no longer so weak, and haven't been for a long time, that they simply allow themselves to be beaten! If India is to be free, the women have to be liberated first!'

In spite of all his achievements, Gandhi was not exactly a feminist. According to his viewpoint, the role of the woman in the freedom struggle was to be limited to assisting and sideline activities. They should decorate strike locations, distribute propaganda material and attend gatherings—he explicitly excluded women's participation in the salt march of 1930 for example. In his world view, the female being was limited to sacrificing itself to the heart of the family. Nonetheless, Gandhi exuded a very powerful attraction for radically feminist women who participated in the struggle more intensely than he and the other men of the independence movement could ever have considered possible. The first opportunity for Indian women to prove their ability and courage was heralded by the turbulent year 1930 when almost all the men of the movement were arrested. 'Most of us menfolk were in prison, and then something remarkable happened,' Jawaharlal Nehru writes in *The Discovery of India* in 1946. 'Our women came to the front and took charge of the struggle. Women had always been there, of course, but now there was an avalanche of them, which took not only the British government but their menfolk by surprise. Here were these women—women of the upper middle classes, leading sheltered lives in their homes; peasant women; working-class women; rich women—pouring out in their tens of thousands in defiance of government order ... It was not only the display of courage and daring, but what was even more surprising was the organisational power they showed.'

Nehru and many other members of Congress had, as socialists, grown more open to feminist ideas and demands. Feminism furnished them with the opportunity of trumping the British in terms of progressiveness. Consequently, many concrete measures for the emancipation of women were in fact motivated by reasons other than solely empowering women. Nonetheless, the female comrades in the movement profited from them. Some even attained a certain prominence and respected position. Sarojini Naidu, for example, was elected president of the Congress Party in 1925. Rani Laxmibai Rajwade headed a branch of the National Planning Committee and, in 1927, Margaret Cousins founded the All India Women's Conference. To that circle also belonged a woman by the name of Mridula Sarabhai, who fully blossomed as a radical feminist in these times of political change. Gandhi, who had known Mridula as a seven-year-old girl, once said about her: 'If I had one hundred women like Mridula, I could bring about a complete social revolution.' For Fearless Nadia, roughly the same age, the life of Mridula Sarabhai provided a wealth of politically realistic inspiration.

The Model Mridula

Mridula Sarabhai grew up as the eldest of eight brothers and sisters in an anglicized, very liberal family. Her father was a well-to-do textile factory owner in Ahmedabad who regarded himself as a political rebel; her mother was a follower of the Montessori education method. There was also an aunt in the house who had close connections with the Workers' Movement and the Suffragettes in England. The progressive climate in her parental home boosted Mridula's self-confidence from childhood. At the age of seventeen, she gave her first public address in which she condemned every form of social discrimination between men and women. As a step towards emancipation for the women of Gujarat, she recommended that from now on girls, unmarried women and widows were to be addressed as 'shrimati'. The humiliating titles of other forms of address should be radically eliminated along with the rigorous clothing and jewellery traditions which defined a woman's family status in a manner visible to all. Married women were to wipe the red bindi mark from their foreheads and lay down their bracelets; widows were to wear bright saris again and wash their hair. Women, Mridula found, placed far too much importance on their outer image, on clothing, jewellery and cosmetics. Since she herself, as a matter of principle, wore only the simple cotton cloths that had more or less become the uniform of the freedom movement, it was her personal aim to lay aside all feminine characteristics that could hinder the path to emancipation.

When she was arrested for the first time at the age of twenty-one, she wrote in her prison diary:

> Shyness, softness, helplessness, dependency, lady-like manners ... I don't want to be a doll for show either for men or for society. I don't want to be artificial, unnatural ... I have tried to keep away from the so-called womanly qualities and tried to cultivate certain manly qualities which I consider essential for a woman—desire for adventure, daringness, self-confidence, discipline, ability to do one's work, control one's mind and emotions; one's physique and way of walking should be that of a soldier.[11]

Mridula perceived herself as a soldier of the freedom movement and was regarded as the 'masculine girl-pupil of the Mahatma'. As a teenager, she became a member of the Congress youth movement 'Yuvak Sangh' that encouraged young girls through tutorials and lectures towards more independence and political engagement. Mridula's considerable organizational talent developed while not detracting from her infectious manner. At the age of twenty-three, Mridula sought more concrete tasks and, along with some like-minded ladies in 1934, founded the legendary women's self-help organization 'Jyoti Sangh' in her father's bungalow. Mahatma Gandhi, the guest of honour, laid the foundation stone. This group had tremendous success: Jyoti Sangh educated female social

---

[11] Basu, Aparna, *Mridula Sarabhai, Rebel With a Cause*, 1997.

workers in Ahmedabad who returned to their villages after their training period. At Jyoti Sangh, they had learned to weave, how to make soap and hair oil, and how vegetables are pickled. Some were instructed in printing techniques or furniture production, and sport instruction was part of the programme too. Armed with the tools required for greater economic self-sufficiency, they went back to the women who had remained at home. Mridula was of the firm conviction that economic independence is an essential prerequisite for the progress of women. The centre soon came to be known in the whole country as a refuge for women in trouble as well: beaten wives, children, widows, persecuted women—all were helped pragmatically. An extremely mobile and independent woman, Mridula was not one to rest on her laurels. After a few years with the centre in Ahmedabad, she set off on a mission that lasted several years, travelling from village to village as an educator, activist and teacher, spreading the ideas of Jyoti Sangh during extended sojourns.

Nadia undertook a similar mission in *Bambaiwali*. Wadia Movietone announced the new thriller quite boldly in the newspapers: 'Hush! Nadia is coming—the woman who makes men blush! In a picture that establishes new standards of manhood for men and a new career for women. Fearless Nadia as Bambaiwali keeps the torch of womanhood burning, diffusing the light of Love, Equality and Freedom in the Domestic Domain.'

Educating Amazons

In the film, Nadia runs a village school for women that bears the proud name 'New India'. The teaching programme, of which mainly the gymnastic lessons are shown, has an ideological impetus that is presented in the form of song: 'Wake up, you bright ones!/ India's women are rising up at last./ We are leaving the home and taking to the streets./ Fighters for freedom step onwards, have no fear./ We are ready to march and show our saris evoke freedom./ We're taking the first step./ We hold hands and step onwards.'

Like Mridula Sarabhai in the course of her mission, Nadia arrives in the film village as an intellectual outsider, free from money worries and full of zest. She lives alone in a swish little garden house with flower beds outside the window. The women's centre is next door and it attracts, above all, the young daughters of the town. They wear white shirts and black shorts as their school uniform, swing swords through the air in ballet formations and when they return home they apparently no longer serve their brothers and fathers quite as devotedly as Indian men expect from their wives and daughters. At the beginning of the film, a group of incensed men lament this fact and decide that nothing but a good beating will bring the impertinent women to reason. Then, a property speculator enters the picture and wants to build a new estate on the land of a young widow. Her feisty son asks Nadia for help. Nadia sets off to do just that but is rudely put in her place by the circle of men: as a woman she has no right sticking her nose into this sort of business! As a political activist regarded with suspicion, she has to handle this first fight scene alone, with only 'Gunboat', her pet German Shepherd, to assist with a few strategically inflicted bites. 'We must watch out, something bad is bound to happen,' Nadia later warns the widow and her small son.

Bambaiwali, 1941

The film then relates in great detail how a band of men forms around the property speculator and the elders of the village, against the progressive women's alliance. As befits the customary cinema stereotypes, in *Bambaiwali*, the men of the village are dazzled and seduced by the promises of quick money, while the women keep the long-term perspectives in sight. The conflict intensifies, Nadia is kidnapped, and miraculously freed, and the women of the village go on a general strike. In response to this, the men do not know what to do other than demanding the closure of Nadia's school with the support of an officer. Flanked by two young protégés, Nadia refutes this threat proudly and boldly: 'The men treat us like toys or servants. We had to adopt extreme measures although we didn't plan to originally. But it is not yet too late for a reconciliation. We do not want to neglect the household; housework is part of our natural tasks. We only ask for equal treatment in all important decisions. In the struggle for freedom we want to sit side by side with the men and not be condemned to silence!'

Bambaiwali wouldn't be a Nadia film if her words alone led the argumentative men to agree with her. Weary and somewhat helpless, they toe the line only after Nadia explains to them that their wives will return only if they are treated as equals. In the meantime, the pupils, who at the start of the film were performing a kind of water ballet on dry ground, transform under Nadia's guidance into bold amazons. When at last the men comprehend that the property speculator is planning the downfall of the entire village, it is Nadia's pupils, on horseback, swords in hand, who banish the rogue and his helpers in the film's impressive finale. In a triumphal procession, the women—

strengthened in every aspect and now admired by the men—return to their families as the film draws to an end.

The success of their respective missions was not the only point in common between Mridula and Nadia. In Mridula Sarabhai's archive, there are some letters from husbands that could well have been responses to Nadia's efforts in *Bambaiwali*. Lots of them thank the activist for the education that had revolutionized their family life. Through Mridula's influence, submissive women had transformed into comrades who shared happiness and trouble on equal terms. In *Bambaiwali*, Nadia did just about the same thing.

No Fear of Bosses!

During her life, Mridula enjoyed a friendly relationship not only with Gandhi but also with Jawaharlal Nehru and other prominent personalities in the Congress Party of those years. Had she desired it, a career at the very top of the party would have been hers. But Mridula always remained a rebel who preferred to work at the grass roots and, if necessary, sharply criticize the men in the leading positions. When, for example, in 1936 the Congress Working Committee decided not to admit any women in their ranks, she wrote to Gandhi: 'Congressmen are not interested in understanding the attitudes and views of women who are taking part in public life. In politics, women stand by the Congress, but it is not sympathetic to their social and economic problems. We are loyal Congress women and feel the Congress is the only organisation through which our women's problems can be solved.' Mridula didn't make things easy for the often chauvinistic men in the party. She insisted to the party's head that men hostile to women should be dropped from leading positions and didn't mince her words even if her opponent was admired by the masses.

Nadia's trademark too was this uncompromising attitude and fearlessness towards authorities. This demanded a strength that apparently eschewed teamwork. Both women are leaders by nature who surround themselves with assistants, helpers and admirers rather than with equal partners of either sex. This hierarchy which seemed natural—in Nadia's case developed afresh each time in the cinematic concept—was created by Mridula Sarabhai in the course of her travels through the country. On her own initiative, for years she went from one flashpoint to the next, always battling her way to the frontline. In the 1930s and 1940s, she established a legendary reputation as a negotiator in conflicts between Hindus and Muslims, but above all for taking up the cause of women suppressed by feudal lords, moneylenders or violent husbands. Much like Nadia's reputation in *Hunterwali*, it was sometimes simply enough to mention Mridula's name, as in the case of a pimp who tortured a girl, and kept her in a brothel against her will. Mridula sent round a co-worker—that was all it took to scare the man: he released the girl immediately.

Following the partition of India, Mridula manoeuvred her way into the region of Punjab. The division of the subcontinent into India and Pakistan led to a dramatic mass exodus in the region: an estimated twelve million people lost their homes. On both sides, Hindu and Muslim fanatics tried to outdo each other with acts of cruelty, one massacre leading to the next. Survivors had to undergo myriad humiliations: a widespread form of dishonouring the enemy was the kidnapping of young women to force them into marriage with a partner of the other religion.

Mridula, with a female voluntary corps, had specialized in finding such women, freeing them from the clutches of their kidnappers and reuniting them with their families in camps. In spite of the courage involved, their spectacular exploits were not uncontroversial. By the time Mridula knocked at the door as liberator, some of the women had long since resigned themselves to their fate, others had perhaps willingly changed sides in the hope of an improvement in their situation. Mridula never wavered—she fought a losing battle for six years, her groundbreaking work eliciting contradictory responses. While many prominent politicians distanced themselves from Mridula Sarabhai, she enjoyed great respect among people who were also Nadia fans: workers, peasants—the simple folk. Mridula and Nadia stood uncompromisingly and energetically at the side of these people, whether in real life or on the screen.

Beauty and Brawn

On a visit to a women's university in Bombay shortly after she became the prime minister of India in 1966, Indira Gandhi gave a lecture on the curious paradox encapsulated in the fact that India had produced many strong women in an extremely patriarchal society:

> In few countries do women hold higher position in politics and public life than in India. But this should not lead us to think that the old inequalities and disabilities from which the women of India suffered have all ended. Ours is a country in which oppositions and contradictions thrive, and nowhere is this more so than as regards women. If we have women who

> are among the most progressive in the world, we also have women who are among the most backward. In law, all discrimination between man and woman has been abolished. Yet, we all know the social and economic hardships which our women suffer in addition to the general hardships ... in a society so poor and still so largely mediaeval as ours. ... In India, in spite of the fact that the emancipation of women has released powerful social forces, non-acceptance of equality of women on the part of men is a great hurdle.[12]

On-screen, Fearless Nadia belonged without a doubt to the most progressive women of her time, incorporating one side of the typically Indian contrast. Even if her films seem somewhat dated at present, Nadia's natural feminism was forward-looking and is a source of inspiration to this day. For example, whenever a supposedly normal course of action was suggested to her by men around her—a father, a suitor, the village elders, the villain—Nadia simply brushed these aside with her enchanting laughter. This was the way she reacted to marriage proposals, admonishments, offers to surrender or attempted intimidation. She fought in an unorthodox manner—as befitting the situation on hand—and didn't run the risk of entanglement with bureaucracy thereby. It is particularly noticeable how she shows solidarity with women who, strictly speaking, do not belong to her social class, when she—as in most films—plays a woman of privilege, an academic or a daughter from a well-to-do home.

---

[12] Masani, Zareer, *Indira Gandhi, A Biography*, London: Hamish Hamilton, 1976

As opposed to many intellectual feminists in real life, Nadia had no difficulty in building a bridge to women who wouldn't define themselves with the word. She is always shown as a person who can certainly talk in public, but has more up her sleeve. Just like the countless women in India who perform heavy physical work, Nadia possessed immense strength of body—a feature that isn't generally considered typically feminine and was not at all at one with the delicate feminine ideal of beauty. She turns this apparent flaw to her advantage by directly displaying her body and putting her talents to extensive use. According to the Indian film studies expert Neela Karnik, who has been studying the reactions of female audiences in India for several years, lots of women viewers identified with the heroine Nadia on a psychologically sexual level. In everyday India, it is expected that women in the fields or in the factory perform the same work as men. In her film roles, Nadia displays the same traits as a woman among men—in fights, in crisis and extreme situations. Women of the middle and upper classes interviewed by Neela Karnik felt repelled by these abilities and developed impulsive machinations of dissociation. Other women liked this very athletic, acrobatic and fantastic exaggeration of feminine powers. For peasants, factory workers or underprivileged housewives, Nadia represented a woman with whom they shared an intangible affinity and whose physical attributes they could relate to and be proud of.

Housewife and Vigilante

Film producers in India reacted to the Nadia phenomenon with a curious blindness: come independence, self-confident women gradually disappeared from the screen. Conservative men dominated the business and limited themselves to making films which corresponded to the taste of traditional men. The fact that film heroines depicted as strong have a huge market potential, and not only for a female public, was simply ignored. Years ran into decades and still Nadia didn't appear to have any successor, until at last Doordarshan landed a huge hit in 1985 with *Rajani.* Each episode of the series narrated minor, not always particularly credible, crusades of the resolute housewife Rajani against the everyday scourges that make life difficult for middle-class Indian women. She would hunt down a devious astrologer one day and then follow it up with a campaign against a corrupt gas-delivery man, or a foxy pickpocket in a bus, or, in one of the most celebrated episodes, go hammer and tongs at errant taxi drivers. When she discovers that the husband of her maidservant beats his wife and wants to marry another woman, Rajani energetically makes him see reason. Reviews—for example in the *Sunday Observer*—found Rajani too masculine, too brash and too undiplomatic in her dealings. On the other hand, Meena Kaushik, a sociologist and market researcher in Bombay, interviewed viewers who were part of the newly discovered female middle class. They were all enthusiastic at having a rabid housewife as a heroine. Meena Kaushik summarized the results of her study: 'Rajani provides a catharsis for those women who live very suppressed lives and who are not permitted to voice their opinion. I think she is a harbinger of change.'

In the 1980s, Bollywood also tried to find a way out of popular cinema's identity crisis with the help of heavily armed angels of vengeance—the male superheroes seemed to have lost their appeal with the Indian public which was looking for something new. Someone who helped set the style of the angry young woman character was Dimple Kapadia. The actress had become an overnight star at the age of fourteen with *Bobby*. Soon after, she married Rajesh Khanna and quit films. After ten years of marriage and two children, Dimple dared a comeback as a divorced woman. That in itself was considered sensational. In quite a few films after her comeback, she can be seen in skin-tight latex outfits, kilos worth of ammunition wrapped round her chest, small daggers adorning her hips, machine gun in hand. In *Zakhmi Aurat*, she plays the head of a women's gang of rape victims. Their mission's creed is: castrate the perpetrators! The mixture of rousing stories, glamour combined with sex and violence was quite a commercial success for a while.

The gun-wielding wild beauties obviously provided a refreshing contrast for the audience to the weepy, helpless film ladies of the 1960s and 1970s. But there was a catch. In 1987, Utthara Kumari described the phenomenon in the *Indian Express* of 13 March: while this new character could shoot, throw bombs and murder just as well as her male colleagues, she didn't seem to enjoy it. 'She is always ready to drop the combative facade and melt into the arms of the hero. This avenging angel, then, is hardly different from the heroine hovering in the background.' The journalist believed that while it was certainly necessary to bring strong female figures to the cinema, this new breed of heroine didn't fulfil feminist demands. She found better examples in Indian film history: 'There was Nadia, the stunt queen. But she was genuine. She fought all her battles on her own on the celluloid. She was called the fearless Nadia. And rightly so! Whereas today's heroines whimper and simmer with fear beneath the bravado. They have no real guts. They wear boots and hold guns alright but there the illusion stops. Do we really need such tough women? One thing is certain: we don't want any heroines who just serve to provide glamour. This doesn't mean we want the other extreme—a superwoman who flexes her muscles and bares her teeth. So, one has to strike a balance.'

Fashioning Legends

It was also in the mid-1980s that two Indian women hit the headlines, heroines of the everyday, who filled the gaps as bearers of Nadia's bequest: the policewoman Kiran Bedi and the legendary bandit Phoolan Devi.

Kiran Bedi, born in 1949, was India's first policewoman to attain the highest echelons of the state's bureaucratic apparatus. An ambitious, liberal father, a first-class education and an early career as a tennis player had equipped Kiran Bedi with the necessary confidence for such a position. When she was still new to the job, the press became interested in her when she had Indira Gandhi's wrongly parked car towed away. She garnered her first laurels in west Delhi for tackling the traffic chaos and for a reform programme to deal with local gang terror. With the help of small bank loans and an estate agent, Kiran Bedi transformed notorious smugglers into decent citizens. She gave talks in prisons, opened several drug rehabilitation centres and gained a reputation as an incorruptible, effective policewoman. Media conscious, she didn't let any opportunity slip by for making a spectacular appearance. When an American journalist asked her about her not entirely uncontroversial work ethic, she had this to say: 'When I started out I didn't wait to see if the men would accept my order. I just gave it.'[13]

While Kiran Bedi's police fervour had a much more palpable effect on the state than Nadia's political engagement on-screen, the image of the younger policewoman certainly resembled Nadia's screen presence. Both are stylized self-made women who displayed a remarkable degree of self-confidence to rigorously and determinedly claim a place of their own in the male-dominated social arena—a space that simply didn't exist before them. Kiran Bedi made incorruptibility her trademark and, like Nadia, impressed with her courageous, feisty confrontations with superiors and authorities. There were similarities in sartorial preferences too: both enjoyed creating an 'eccentric' wardrobe with the help of little arty flourishes to practical trouser suits. Nadia liked frills, ribbons, embroidery, while Kiran Bedi combined her uniform with unusual earrings and high-heeled boots, which made her look like a fantasy policewoman from a Hindi film.

The largest-selling women's magazine in India, *Femina*, did features on the unusual policewoman and her family situation on several occasions. Kiran Bedi lived with her parents who managed the housework for her. Since her husband didn't want to leave his farm in Amritsar they only saw each other twice a year. 'My husband knew he was marrying a very ambitious career-oriented woman. He's not willing to sacrifice his career for me, and I'm not willing to sacrifice mine for him. It's as simple as that. Just because I am a woman—am I supposed to sacrifice? I said

[13] Bumiller, Elisabeth, *May You Be the Mother of a Hundred Sons*, London: Penguin Books, 1990.

to him: "I'll have a second child only on the condition that you be here and you participate." But he said he couldn't move. So we have one child.'

Just to what effect this policewoman mastered her role as an idol ready to fight is illustrated not least by the general support she received in a spectacular trial. In 1988, a lawyer who had been caught picking pockets was produced in court in handcuffs by an overzealous policeman. Kiran Bedi, as the superior of the policeman, refused to suspend him from duty, thereby making herself the number one enemy of the Indian lawyers' consortium. Followed closely by the media down to the last detail, the case reached the Supreme Court.

The second Indian rebel of the decade who attained international fame, and who could be seen as having taken up Nadia's mantle, was the bandit queen Phoolan Devi who attained notoriety with the Behmai massacre where she shot dead twenty young Thakur men, allegedly in retaliation for the killing of her lover and her own rape and humiliation two years ago. When she gave herself up to the police in 1983 in a remarkable ceremony, there was a list of sixty-six crimes she was accused of: murder, robbery, plundering and kidnapping.

An interesting parallel to Fearless Nadia can be found in the forming of a legend around Phoolan Devi prior to her surrender. Shocked but also fascinated, all the Indian newspapers had reported on the Behmai massacre in detail. The deed went on to become part of folklore, described and sung of in folk songs and comic books. The horror of the bloody act was mixed with sensationalist lust. Phoolan Devi's deeds weren't simply viewed in the context of her life story. Since there was not a single photo of her, an artist drew an attractive phantom portrait from the description of eyewitnesses. The portrait started the myth of a beautiful bandit, greedy for sexual excesses in the jungle. At the time of the Behmai killings, Phoolan Devi's hair had long since been closely shorn and she wore, as was usual amongst bandits, a police uniform as disguise. Yet the picture people had of her was quite different. The German travel magazine *Merian* wrote, for example, in 1982 that with her 'well-rounded bottom and full breasts', Phoolan Devi deliberately made men 'lust after her'. The number of her affairs would certainly be worthy of a place in the *Guinness Book of Records* if only someone knew their exact number. Former bandit friends in prison were asked in detail about the spicy details of living with Phoolan Devi and they responded voluntarily: 'Other girls were just as tomboyish as Phoolan, but maintained a certain restraint in the presence of men. They would go behind trees or bushes to get washed. Not so Phoolan: she'd undress in front of everyone as though no one was there. The others also spoke somewhat like other women. Phoolan is the dirtiest whore I have ever known. When she opens her mouth, filth and swear words come out.'

Nadia's resort to violence on the screen—mostly limited to fisticuffs which seldom ended in death—may have been less brutal than that of Phoolan Devi, yet the erotic component certainly played an important role in the way her fans accepted her as a fighting machine. A good-looking woman seems to make the use of violence easier to accept on-screen. Likewise, the imaginary beauty of the unknown bandit queen served as a vehicle to weigh up the crimes symbolically, and to understand Phoolan Devi as an avenger with noble motives. A correspondent of the magazine *Sunday* wrote for example: 'She was extraordinary because there existed a sadness in the story of her life: the feeling that a terrible injustice had been inflicted on her. For this reason her crime against the twenty men in Behmai was simultaneously regarded as an act of salvation. For a moment she was identical to any Indian woman who had been raped, humiliated and treated like dirt, and there was the feeling that she was less a murderer than a woman who had fought for her rights.'

The media had turned Phoolan Devi into a lady Robin Hood, a justified avenger following in the footsteps of Fearless Nadia as Hunterwali. Phoolan Devi apparently knew these projections, judging by the manner she gave herself up—together with her consort Man Singh Yadav and twenty-two other bandits—in a self-directed ceremony on 12 February 1983. With a red woollen shawl over her khaki uniform, a red scarf tied round her black hair, she stepped on to the specially erected rostrum. She laid down her 315 Mauser and her ammunition belt in front of images of the goddess Durga and Mahatma Gandhi. An enormous crowd of onlookers cheered her as the 'bandit queen' fell to her knees in front of the Home Secretary, kissing his feet as a sign of submission, and placed a garland of flowers around his neck. But Phoolan Devi didn't entirely throw herself into the role she had taken on through this solemn occasion. In the storm of flashbulbs, she cursed all the photographers and journalists with colourful vocabulary. They reacted bitterly and grumpily that Phoolan Devi didn't fulfil the ideal of a 'bandit beauty' in real life. She vanished from sight for some years in prison, where she got her way when she insisted she be accommodated together with Man Singh in the men's wing.

In the meantime, Shekar Kapur decided to make a film of Phoolan Devi's story. His primary concern wasn't the authenticity of the story, but the depiction of a higher truth and the condemning of the caste system, Kapur said in an interview in 1994. *Bandit Queen* wasn't controversial in India because of its faithfulness to truth; it was the generous naked scenes that caused a stir. Almost coinciding with the international film premiere of *Bandit Queen* in Cannes, came Phoolan Devi's release under surveillance and bail. The legend lived again. On account of her popularity among the lower castes, she was immediately courted by different political parties. Though initially reluctant, Phoolan Devi came to realize how useful this could be for her own interests as well. In 1996, she eventually stood as parliament candidate for the Samajvadi Party, a so-called socialist outfit. And here the commonality with Nadia comes full circle—although critics reproached Phoolan Devi that her political statements were wishy-washy and lacking precision, among the exploited, beaten and raped, she commanded respect for standing firmly and energetically at the side of those in need.

What Nadia demonstrated to her fans in film after film matches the message that Phoolan Devi passed on at election events or in women's magazines until her death in 2001: 'I'm working for the improvement of living conditions of poor and exploited women and children. Sometimes girls come to me with stories of suffering from their married life. I don't leave these girls on their own. I fight for them. I fight for the rights of all women.'

8

HUMAN GODS

Tigress, 1947

With 330 million gods to search from, it is not easy to find one's way around the pantheon of the Hindu deities. Curious passers-by, however, have plentiful opportunities to gain at least a passing insight into the alien world of gods—by visiting, for example, the many street vendors selling calendars, posters and postcards with images of the gods. Harmoniously rubbing shoulders with Jesus or the blue-skinned flute-playing Krishna at such roadside stalls, are Leonardo DiCaprio and the top stars of current Bollywood productions. At a second glance, you recognize that amongst the Hindu gods there are apparently some best-selling favourites whose popularity cannot merely be explained by the hierarchy in the pantheon. The monkey-god Hanuman, for example, enjoys a large fan following, as does gentle Lakshmi or the elephant-headed Ganesh. The pleasant mixture in the vendors' stands reflects the lack of a dogmatic teaching in Hinduism and leads the German professor of religion Peter Antes to depict Hinduism as 'a kind of supermarket of religious goods that has something in stock even for the most unusual taste'. Female gods, signifying the personifications of the feminine Shakti and supposed to have existed before the male gods, are another favourite with the vendors. In particular, the goddess Durga who is an important subject of research in female cult figures in India—be it in cinema or in politics.

Hinduism is a religion truly compatible with cinema. In contrast to the Christianity of the New Testament, the religious material available with Hinduism is well suited for film adaptation because the gods—like the Greek gods—have very human qualities. They are jealous, make mistakes, drink, gamble, love and hate one another, have children, turn into people and conduct wars. Moreover, the ancient stories of the Ramayana, the Puranas and the Mahabharata provide a veritable treasure trove of legends and fables with apt morals with which people all over the country are in some way acquainted and with which they identify. In short, dramaturgs can sink their teeth into this rich abundance of material.

D.G. Phalke recognized the film potential of Indian mythology that was kept alive into the twentieth century, above all by folk theatre and dances. The stage could, however, show the miracles and bold transformations of the gods only symbolically in a manner that bears comparison to the Brechtian alienation effect. It certainly didn't help that it was mostly neighbours or acquaintances who slipped into the costumes of gods in the folk theatre. In cinema on the other hand, actors who were not known personally to the public represented the gods and what they did on-screen was a concrete visualization of what had until then remained in the imagination of the believers. The film gods effortlessly steered their heavenly carriages through the skies, animals could speak and the dead came back to life, flaming discuses were sent flying and figures could appear out of thin air and disappear likewise. So it's not surprising that the Hindu world of gods was brought to life completely afresh through cinema. In the era of silent movies, 70 per cent of all Indian films were so-called 'mythologicals' in which the lives of gods and holy people were told. Correspondingly, the public transformed the cinema hall into a kind of religious cult location. The public bowed respectfully to the screen gods and, just as in the temple proper, threw coins at the screen as a sign of respect—rituals that are still occasionally practised today.

Queen of the Beasts

The Fearless Nadia films are a world away from the rather ceremonial, somewhat theatrical genre of the mythological. But certain elements of Nadia's screen image would nonetheless have reminded her fans of the religious emblems of the epics: above all, Nadia's ability to appear at the right place at the right time and her stunts that defy gravity and great distance. The daring costumes are also reminiscent of the erotic dress of the gods. As inspiration for her costumes, Nadia usually took European and American fashion magazines to the tailor's, yet the result was—as so often in her career—a Western–Indian amalgam. In *Tigress*, for example, it appears that fashionable 5th Avenue leopard costumes have been tropically shortened and the end result resembles the elegant loin cloth, the trademark of Shiva. The *Tigress* costume turned Nadia into a half-animal, half-human figure, a common form of appearance of Indian gods on earth.

In *Jungle Princess*, Nadia's god-like qualities are not limited to accessories. It is an adventure film set in Nigeria inspired by the American 'Tarzan' films. The main attractions are the wild animals of the jungle, some of which are Nadia's closest friends. The humanizing of animals have been part of the repertoire of cinematic tradition from the earliest days of silent movies, and at the same time is an important element of the drama of Indian epics which abound in speaking monkeys and apes, golden swans as marriage brokers and much more. In *Jungle Princess*, Nadia bears the name 'Mala' which at least indirectly can be understood as a play on the Mahabharata king 'Nala', especially as they both rule in inaccessible jungle areas. Africa, in the film, is not only—as in comparable colonial films from the

West—a backdrop for exotic adventure; it's also a place that recalls the mythological, pre-civilization age of the Indian epics.

Jungle Princess, 1942

The prologue recounts Nadia's arrival in Africa as a child, cast up on the lonely shores as the sole survivor of a dramatic shipwreck. From there, she makes her way into the jungle to learn its ways, all alone in the world, doll clasped beneath her arm. She encounters all sorts of wild animals, screeching birds, cheeky monkeys and rampaging elephants which frighten her at first. But before long Nadia can be seen playing happily with two small lion cubs. Twenty years later, when the action proper begins, both Nadia and the lion cubs have grown up. Nadia, in a black, low-cut mini-dress, resides in a palatial cave and has matured into queen of the lions. Like Durga who is continuously portrayed as riding on a lion, Nadia forms a close community with the big cats. She lives with them and they communicate as though there were no problems of understanding between man and beast. The humanized lions act as her helpers, protectors and underlings who recognize Nadia as their queen—thereby raising her to the rank of a god on earth.

For all her love of animals, Nadia initially refused to take part in the risky undertaking, but once again Homi managed to persuade her. He had engaged a troupe of neutered lions and a tamer from a circus and the stage was a huge cage disguised as a cave. During the preparations, Homi was the first person in the team to get close to the big cats. That in itself was not sufficient to convince Nadia. It was only when a small circus girl joined the animals with a bowl of milk that her ambition was fired. But Nadia remained aware of the enormous risk throughout filming. During an early rehearsal, a lioness hadn't seen the bars behind the jungle backdrop and in a surprise leap over Nadia found her head lodged between the bars. In response, the other lions started a terrible roar and approached Nadia and the cameraman with nervously twitching tails. The tamer saved the situation, brought the actors with shaking knees to safety and freed the lioness. 'It was a moment of pure fear,' Nadia reported, 'and what followed for me was the most alarming filming I ever did.' With unerring instinct her mother guessed the danger her daughter was putting herself in. She gave Nadia hell: 'What a terrible daughter you are to your mother! Do you want to die?' Homi Wadia also remembers such comments with a twinge of bad conscience. Thankfully nothing happened, and none of the dramatic events of the making are apparent in the finished film: the audience sees Nadia stroking the lions familiarly, sleeping next to them, sees how they allow her to leap onto their shoulders, and even let her slip her hand into the jaws of the biggest one.

Jungle Princess relates how an Indian expedition embarks on a search for Nadia. The fame of the fearless lion-queen has reached Bombay, where a large residence has been waiting for the rightful heiress ever since the shipwreck. An evil uncle wants to declare the disappeared girl dead to benefit from the riches himself. However, a lawyer of integrity takes up Nadia's case and sends a search group to her legendary kingdom. The Indian delegation in the rainforest behaves as oddly as Europeans or Americans in comparative films, and naturally complicated intrigues, full of drama, abound when they reach the destination. Nadia's evil uncle and the devious mistress of the king want to kill Nadia to get at her money. They surprise Nadia, who had just made herself comfortable on a high tree, with an attack from behind. Nadia falls down, but the shot wasn't fatal. As she writhes bleeding and curled up in pain, the lions come to her aid. With his concerned gaze, one of the lions, Shankar (another name for Shiva), takes on the role of a doctor in the following sequence. 'Help me, Shankar, bring me the healing leaves,' Nadia requests, and off the lion trots. In the undergrowth, he tugs a mighty branch free and brings it to the patient who assures her faithful friend that thanks to his help she will be hale and hearty the next day. There is close-up after close-up of Shankar's compassionate eyes, resting on Nadia, the other lions gathered in a semicircle around the sick woman like a worried family. After this intervention, the film races to an action-packed finale and ends with Nadia's heart-rending departure from the lions as she sets off for Bombay.

In many other Nadia films, the German shepherd dog called 'Gunboat' and the horse 'Punjab Ka Beta' play the main animal roles. Just as Indian gods are closely connected to particular 'vahanas'—for example, Ganesh and his rat, the death god Yama with a buffalo, Lakshmi and her owl, Durga with the lion—Nadia forms a trio with her dog and horse. 'Gunboat' and 'Punjab Ka Beta' were given equal mention with the human actors in the titles, credits and advertising fliers, and enjoyed a similar popularity among the fans. Like 'Lassie' or 'Fury' in Hollywood, Nadia's dog and horse join in the action, snatching pistols from criminals, warning Nadia of danger or rescuing her from tricky situations.

However, since animals are regarded with great respect in the Hindu religion, there were certain differences to the intelligent animals in Western films who were primarily aimed at a young public. It is common knowledge that the belief in reincarnation incorporates the possibility of returning in the next life as an animal. As a result, in India not only cows but in some places monkeys, rats or elephants attain a position of almost cult worship. Nadia's deep love of animals was in any event a facet of her popularity, a helpful vehicle that helped her attain glory as a star. And whoever manages to reach the galaxy of stars in India lives closer to the gods than to mere mortals.

The Big Blow-up

Jungle Princess marked the 'seven-year itch' in Nadia's career. Dark clouds were gathering over Wadia Movietone.

Parallel to the Nadia film, J.B.H. Wadia had produced *The Court Dancer*, the first English-language film from India. The critics were bursting with hymns of praise for this sumptuously produced melodrama in which a prince goes against royal conventions. Listening to the call of his heart, he insists on marrying the enchanting palace dancer. The premiere of the film supplanted even the war news from the front pages of Indian newspapers and Baburao Patel wrote in *Filmindia*, October 1941: 'I salute producer Jamshed Wadia from Wadia Movietone for this pioneering enterprise in producing India's first picture in English: *The Court Dancer*. When this picture goes across the seas to foreign countries, it will be the most eloquent ambassador of our homeland. I know what it is to be an Indian in those arrogant foreign countries where every coloured man is taken for a barbarian. I congratulate all—the director, the technicians, and the artistes—for contributing their best to this excellent enterprise. In the proud smile of the stray and lonely Indian, lost in the foreign country today, will they get the reward of their labour. For, truly, as cultural propaganda, *The Court Dancer* is a patriot's gift to the nation.'

The triumph turned bitter soon after, for it brought the long-simmering conflict between the Wadia brothers to light with a force that made further cooperation impossible. *The Court Dancer* had stretched the studio resources considerably, and during its production brought the studio to the brink of bankruptcy. The film was initially intended to be produced as a bilingual in Hindi and Bengali (the Bengali title was *Raj Nartaki*). As a matter of pride, and with one eye on his place in Indian cinema history, JBH had taken the decision to produce a version simultaneously in the English language. While in actual terms this did not add much to the overall budget, it did eat into the raw stock quota that came into force during the production. But JBH didn't let that disturb him—and from his point of view, the decision proved right once the film was released.

The Court Dancer became a glorious artistic success which to JBH compensated for its failure to recover all its production costs. The Bengali version of the film was declared a commercial success while the Hindi version did poorly. The English version, which was always meant to be an artistic endeavour, surprised many by having a successful run at the Metro Cinema chain nationwide. The aggregate box office returns from all three versions showed a profit. The whole experience encouraged JBH to do what he long had in mind: bring the curtain down over the era of stunt films once and for all. He was simply fed up, he explained in an interview, of writing and producing one film after the other along the tried and tested formula with Nadia as star.

Homi on the other hand was thunderstruck when JBH suggested to him that they terminate the contracts with Nadia and John Cawas. He felt betrayed and jealous when JBH and Hilla shifted all their praise away from him and 'his' star to the new 'dream team' from Calcutta, the Boses. The driving force behind *The Court Dancer* was director Modhu Bose and his beautiful wife Sadhona, a danseuse extraordinaire, and Hilla's cultured alter ego. To Homi's perception it was unfair that Nadia's work—and his—in stunts that had brought the studio such financial success was belittled by JBH at the expense of those Bengalis with their highfalutin 'social films'. Homi vented his anger and stated that JBH was an intellectual snob, egotistical and economically short-sighted to boot. Decades later, he recalls: 'We had a terrible argument. I cajoled JBH: "Let us continue producing both stunt films and social drama, on a two-pronged front." But he remained resolute. He didn't want to do any more Nadia films! I asked him to film at least one more with her, but he refused.'

The conflict wasn't new, but the harshness was. Even though in retrospect everyone who was part of it traces the argument to professional and cinematic differences, a strange, impenetrable fog hangs over the whole story. A Wadia co-worker once mentioned an open argument between Nadia and Hilla, which could have led to the conflict. Even though Homi roundly denies that Nadia interfered in the argument, it does seem plausible that the two women collided. The quarrel did involve Nadia's future, after all. She was thirty-four years old at the time, an advanced age for an Indian actress. From her wages, she, her mother, Bobby and a housekeeper were able to live well in the small flat in Colaba, but they had not saved anything. The uncertain war situation made things worse.

A reconciliation between Homi and JBH was inconceivable for the time being. The Wadia brothers, who apparently didn't exchange a word with one another for seven months, went their separate ways. JBH remained in the studio with bold plans for social dramas. Homi, the junior partner, left Lovji Castle at once, defeated and angry. He didn't have much to pack: he had options on the contracts with Fearless Nadia, John Cawas and some other stunt actors. And a screenplay written by JBH. He also had the Machiavellian backing of M.B. Billimoria who favoured Homi's business acumen to JBH's politically unpopular adventurism. JBH continued to produce films at the Wadia Movietone Studios for some more time until wartime inflation and raw stock quota restrictions made it unviable. He sold the property and equipment to V. Shantaram who renamed the studio Rajkamal Kalamandir. In an act of chauvinism, Shantaram let go of the studio's non-Marathi-speaking staff and restructured the property, tearing down the ancestral Lovji Castle.

The parting of ways came, not coincidentally, at the beginning of the end of the studio era in India. During wartime, an enormous amount of black money was floating around India, laundered in the film industry and elsewhere. In the film industry, this was visible in the growing number of producers without fixed abodes. These freelance producers hired everything—from the cameraman to the lighting technician and the extras, workers and the equipment as well as the studio—on individual film contracts which were terminated once the film was complete. Besides, there were increasing shortages in the availability of raw materials which rendered the long-term planning of the studios almost obsolete. Inflation also made it tough for the large film businesses to function with their huge infrastructure. The host of employees, the canteens, zoos and libraries could no longer be financed.

Wadia Movietone was not the only studio to disintegrate. In 1947, Bombay Talkies declared themselves bankrupt. Prabhat avoided closure until 1953 when the studio era was practically long since a thing of the past. The effects of the restructuring are reflected in the production figures of the same year: of sixty-one films produced in Bombay, only forty came from well-known studios.

The only ones to really profit from this restructuring were the star actors. With the end of the studio era, their names alone stood for a certain style, for success and quality—and they were paid handsomely for this. The share of star fees in the total production costs reached astronomical proportions in the early 1940s. Simple employees with a monthly salary had transformed into key figures on whose power and moods the producers had to rely increasingly.

One of the first actresses in India to recognize the way the wind was blowing was the eccentric Mukhtar Begum. This impression is garnered from a story the cameraman Krishna Gopal has to tell. One fine day, Mukhtar Begum didn't appear on set, with no explanation—which in 1939 was an abomination for an actress. The team waited for hours until Krishna Gopal and the director set off to look for her and discovered Mukhtar Begum in her dressing room. She was sitting perfectly at ease in front of the mirror, putting the final touches to her make-up while the screenplay writer Agha Hashr Kashmiri lay on the carpet, reading her dialogues out loud. Kashmiri, known as the 'Shakespeare of India', was regarded as one of the most important men in theatre at that time. He grinned smugly when the two men stopped short in the doorway and said: 'Regard this lady, trying in despair to add a little more glamour to her face—as though anyone is going to be looking at her when they hear my words.' Mukhtar Begum got up silently, walked to where Kashmiri lay, and placed her foot on his chest. 'Regard this Indian Shakespeare: he humbly wriggles beneath the heel of the great Mukhtar Begum,' she said.

For Nadia, a typical product of the studio age, Homi's departure from Wadia Movietone meant that she was faced with an abrupt end to her career. Even when Homi urged her to make her name as an actress in social drama, it was as clear as day to her that she, as the queen of the now somewhat old-fashioned genre, wouldn't make the leap into the new star system. She also knew how closely entwined her career was with the best stunt director of India—and found his well-meant advice hurtful. Even if she wasn't the sort to easily panic, her despair was palpable.

Her old problem—the excess weight—reared its head once more and her consumption of alcohol rose alarmingly. To forget all her troubles and the gloomy outlook for the future, Nadia went out a lot—and not just with Homi. This provided further grist to rumour mongers, vindicating those who had gleaned enjoyment from haranguing her about her circus past. The fact that Bobby was being spoken of as a troublemaker in teenage circles at this very time could hardly have relieved Nadia's misery though it provided gossip columnists with perfect material. On the recommendation of her mother, Nadia eventually decided to look the end of her film career bravely in the face. She took on an apprenticeship in 'Flory's Hairdressing Salon'. Somehow, the family and the housekeeping had to be financed after all and a new daily routine established. In those dark months in which Nadia acquainted herself with redolent waves, curlers, and peroxide, and with hairstyles currently in vogue in Paris, she was seldom in the mood for romantic weekends in the beach hut at Juhu. The relaxed parties with friends, where they played, laughed and danced, no longer happened. Her relationship with Homi grew distinctly chilled.

The Birth of Basant Pictures

After the break with JBH, Homi had problems of his own. He was determined to make films according to his vision with which he would not perhaps win laurels in the history of film but with which he could make money. This interest united him with his trusted colleagues from the Wadia Movietone days, Babubhai Mistri and Nanabhai Bhatt. Without the Lovji Castle studio, they were not only unemployed but also in a certain sense homeless. The first business meetings between the three men took place in a park, always beneath the same tree. It was spring in Bombay, the time of the Basant festival, and it didn't take them long to decide to continue working as a team under the banner of Basant Pictures. First, they rented a tiny office for ten rupees a month where the small group busied itself with the preparation of a new film. There was, of course, that screenplay Homi had been permitted to take as his share from the old studio. *Mouj* was its title, a contemporary drama about multiple and unrequited love between landowners and peasants who then suddenly come into a large inheritance. A pragmatic sort, Homi opted for the most obvious option: he offered Nadia the second lead role, a somewhat unpleasant femme fatale who almost becomes a marriage wrecker. Cast alongside her was Pahari Sanyal, a star on whose status Homi Wadia pinned some hope. The snobbish actor shared the disgust of fine people for the genre of stunt films. Nadia recounted: 'He didn't want to work with me. A stunt actress simply wouldn't fit to this film, he explained to Homi. In addition he said my Hindi was too bad for the role. The fact that I'd been putting in serious effort, was learning like a person possessed, didn't interest him in the slightest. Then came the first day of filming in the rented Central Studios, and he was very arrogant to begin with. That was to change, thankfully, when he saw I was able to deliver a very long dialogue with no problem at all, flawlessly. We becamc good friends.'

Mouj was Nadia's first foray into character acting, and marked a radical departure into scenes she—and her fans—was unaccustomed to. The suspicions of the audience were aroused even as the credits began to roll: the 'Fearless' was dropped from her name; instead, a heart was drawn around one 'a' of Nadia. Then it began to come thick and fast: Nadia had changed into a sentimental, somewhat spinster-like floozy. At the end of the film, before a pastel pink sky, she prevents her young rival Chanda (played by Kaushalya) from committing suicide. With a tear in her eye, she sighs: 'Chanda, do you know, the heart of a woman is like the sky. The sky changes in the autumn. It changes from morning to evening, and like the sky the heart of a woman can change. Like a tender cloud caught up in a storm. Do you know that, Chanda? Do you know what happens then? Then the heart of the sky grows very sad. It weeps. Tears course down from it. No one can stop it. Chanda! Your love to me is so strong and stormy. It has touched my heart. It brings direction to my lost life.' The Nadia fans rebelled, booed. They were horrified. They didn't want to see Nadia weeping as an ageing aunt! As though things weren't complicated enough, *Mouj*, the first film under the banner of Basant Pictures, was a complete flop, a commercial disaster from the word go.

Divine Strategies

Painfully and somewhat shamefully, *Mouj* had confirmed beyond any doubt how cast in iron Nadia's image was. Like the guardian angels and gods, Nadia was allowed to vary her role from film to film, but not to fundamentally change it. This sort of typecasting does exist in Western film history, but not as rigorously as in India. An actress who plays the role of a mother even once, runs the risk of never being able to play the part of a lover again. The same is true for the few actresses who marry, and have children. As soon as these private details leak out to the public, it is considered repugnant and unattractive for these women to depict a bride or lover on-screen.

Cinema in India influences everyday life in a different manner than in any other country. It is more than mere entertainment. Film stars, with the help of numerous magazines and a perfectly coordinated game between advertising, award ceremonies and public appearances, are deified. Young-and-upcoming stars and established legends of cinema smile down from gigantic advertising boards on the chaotic city traffic. Above all, the star cult makes it clear how blurred in the Indian psyche the lines are between the world of films and reality.

The life of stars, their everyday routine, their love life and problems are part of a universe that may have some points of reference to Indian reality, but are also a continuation of the old myths. Nothing enjoys greater popularity in India than the stories of promiscuous Hindu deities that have been repackaged and delivered fresh week after week in the affairs and scandals of the Bollywood stars since the start of the 1940s. 'There were secret relationships back in ancient times, too,' explains superstar Amitabh Bachchan. 'Most of our gods had two wives, after all!'

Amitabh Bachchan was the number one rebel in the Bombay cinema of the 1970s, a screen underdog who took on the world alone and was mostly victorious. At the zenith of his career he acted in so many films simultaneously that he sometimes had to die three times in the same day. Then a serious accident occurred: Bachchan almost died performing a stunt. As he lay in a critical condition in hospital, the whole country went into mourning. Prime Minister Indira Gandhi paid him a personal visit in the hospital. All India Radio gave hourly bulletins on his condition. People fasted and prayed across the length and breadth of the country for his speedy recovery. Bachchan survived, a greater icon than ever before, and his school friend Rajiv Gandhi asked him to stand against an extremely difficult candidate in the 1984 elections. Needless to say, Bachchan won and entered parliament. This change from the fantasy world of cinema into the political arena works so often and so smoothly in India that it is possible to talk of a real pathway between fiction and reality.

Particularly steamy is the coupling of politics and cinema in the state of Tamil Nadu, the second largest film centre after Bombay. The cult star Marudur Gopalamenon Ramachandran, aka MGR, followed his film career by shaping the political fortune of the state as a godlike chief minister from 1977 to 1987. His death unleashed a sense of catastrophe. Thirty-one people killed themselves in the tumult and a vicious war of attrition broke out between his wife Janaki and his erstwhile screen partner Jayalalithaa over who would be his political successor. In a relentless power struggle, Jayalalithaa emerged the stronger and became chief minister in 1991.

Jayalalithaa has been described by her fans as a 'goddess on earth', and she allows herself to be treated accordingly. On the occasion of her forty-fifth birthday, a convoy of 1000 cars embarked in a procession to the ceremony hall; 100 cars were required for her presents alone. Fans tattoo her image on their bodies. Numerous supporters wear her as a tummy-covering portrait. To this day, she ensures countrywide chaos, her capricious policy calling forth one government crisis after another. In a telling comment on the power she wields, *India Today* put her on its cover on 4 May 1998, depicting her in skin-tight trouser suits with a powerful-looking whip in her hand. The affinity to Fearless Nadia and her preferred weapon is obvious.

Chosen to Rule

At the start of the 1940s, the close relationship between cinema and politics in India was at best nebulous. The star system was still new and a mature infrastructure was a prerequisite for producing this alliance. Nonetheless, Nadia's case is an exemplary pointer of what particular qualities and rules of the game were taken into account before an actress could be recognized in the powerful role of a fictive ruler. A comparable strategy has been used since the 1980s in south and South East Asia where scores of widows and daughters of murdered politicians have made it to the top of government and political parties: Benazir Bhutto in Pakistan, Sirimavo Bandaranaike in Sri Lanka, Aung San Suu Kyi in Burma, Corazon Aquino in the Philippines, Khaleda Zia and Hasina Wajed in Bangladesh, Megawati Sukarnoputri in Indonesia and finally Sonia Gandhi in India. It is remarkable to note that the most important qualities, which the successful election campaigns of these women were to incorporate, are visible in Nadia's roles.

As in Nadia films, it is always emergency situations and exceptional national circumstances that push women to act and pick up the gauntlet. In contrast to men who, it is commonly assumed, naturally aspire to positions of power, none of these female politicians grow tired of emphasizing that they had never considered playing such an important role, that in reality they are just normal mothers and homemakers or at least long felt a revulsion to politics. 'Housewife' is what Corazon Aquino wrote, for example, on the application form as candidate for presidency.

The dramatic opening conflict for Nadia in her films is conjured up in the election campaigns of the women politicians through suitable media interventions. This 'people like you and me' syndrome as a confidence-building and sympathy-winning measure goes hand in hand with a deliberate suppressing of concrete party proclamations. On endless campaign journeys, countless hands are shaken and assured with feminine concern that in the case of a victory, the poor and those stripped of their rights would be helped.

The archetypical role of the loving mother who cares for her country's children is fleshed out according to the personality, through careful stylization, into an angel of vengeance, a sister or the bride of the nation. Thus, one reads in a sumptuously illustrated report in the *Life* magazine about Benazir Bhutto's wedding with Asif Zardari: 'Six friends of Benazir's stood up and trilled a song in which they list the conditions Asif must accept if he is to marry Benazir: he mustn't hinder her political career, he must look after the children later when she's travelling on her election campaigns and mustn't stop her from going to prison if she has to. "You must agree," the ladies say, "that Benazir will serve the nation above all else."' When *Newsweek* asked Zardari whether he was in love with his wife, he responded with alacrity: 'Is there anyone who isn't? The whole country is in love with her!'—as though he wanted to publicly voice his willingness to share his wife with Pakistan. And Benazir summarizes in her autobiography that she travelled all through the country after her wedding 'to let the people know I am their sister and always will be and that my marriage will in no way affect my political career'.

In her films, Nadia becomes fate's chosen one through incidents that are in a certain measure supernatural—much like in the case of latter-day politicians. Particularly at election times, rumours abound about signs from a higher power that determined the course of events. With Aung San Suu Kyi, it was Buddha statues that supposedly grew breasts as a sign of an approaching female leader; for Benazir Bhutto it was the apparition of her father one night; and for Corazon Aquino, a message at the coffin of her murdered husband that paved the path to the future.

While many parallels to Nadia's career can be found in the mythology surrounding female political leaders in south and South East Asia, that European women may also be assigned this role remains an Indian speciality. Sonia Gandhi, the widow of Rajiv and daughter-in-law of Indira Gandhi is originally from Orbassano, a suburb of Turin. The mayor there, Graziano Dell'Acqua, can't help but be amazed: 'I doubt whether in Italy a foreigner, and a woman on top of that, would attain the position of head of a party that symbolized the national struggle against foreign rule. That at least a large part of the Indian population entrusts their fate to this woman speaks volumes for Indian tolerance.'

THE DYNASTIC SALVATION

Decisive for the nomination of the female politicians was their close relationship to a deceased hero of the people. It is in the name of the father or the husband that they took up their inheritance. On tribunes, beneath enormous photos of their menfolk, they promised the people that they would honour the political bequest and extend it into the future. The names Aung San, Gandhi, Bhutto, Aquino, Zia and Sukarno sent all party programmes and ideologies fading into oblivion and beneath democratic auspices established a ruling vein, dynastic in nature. Following a comparable principle, Basant Pictures attempted to attach themselves to the great Wadia tradition following their sizeable flop *Mouj*. The title of the proposed film was *Hunterwali Ki Beti* (1943) with Nadia in the double role of mother and daughter.

One day in 1943, Homi Wadia surprised his despondent girlfriend with the good news that he had got the money together for the new film. Just as eight years ago, Homi would direct, and as producer he was able to spark enthusiasm for the project among many other former Wadia Movietone co-workers. The budget was very tight and they had to change studio several times during filming because of dwindling resources. The promised wages soon became 'food money' but no one in the experienced team baled out.

The prologue of the film shows the peaceful rule of Queen Hunterwali. All is well with the world until a shady cousin carries out a putsch, sets the palace alight, takes the beloved queen prisoner and shoots her husband. The little daughter is rescued dramatically by a faithful friend and taken to live in safety with simple peasants. Twelve years later, Hunterwali's daughter has grown into a proud agitator for freedom and justice. Naturally, it is her sole desire to terminate the capricious rule of her tyrannical uncle and to free her mother. For this, Hunterwali's old whip, mask and black boots are dusted off, the horses saddled and the popular old tricks refreshed. The snappy sequel to the original shows Nadia in top form, fresh, laughing and light on her feet. Her stunts are breathtaking and have become even more perfect: she leaps over dangerous chasms, somersaults onto her horse, joins in custard-pie fights enthusiastically, captures her enemies with her whip and clambers up rickety ladders onto propeller planes.

As her own successor, Nadia outdid herself. The public was enthusiastic about the old/new Hunterwali. Just like politicians, Nadia profited from a hoary tradition held high in popular regard, so that she merely had to cite her political intentions to be considered by the public as being on the right side. Nadia's deistic star qualities are signposted in *Hunterwali Ki Beti* even more. Her appearance had a high popular recall, her legendary clothing rekindled sweet cinema memories, and the numerous refined tricks confirmed the well-known image. In contrast to the original, *Hunterwali Ki Beti* was no surprise success, but a calculated, economic necessity for Basant Pictures. It was with relief that Nadia, Homi Wadia and his partners realized that financially their business idea had done better than they had dared hope. The film laid down a solid basis for a new start in a modest studio in the Bombay neighbourhood of Chembur. This land included a hillock, a stream, and acres of open land that provided a perfect rural backdrop for stunt films. On it, Homi initially built a tin shed studio. By 1950, he and

Comet, 1949

Toofani Tirandaz, 1946

JBH were reconciled again. JBH took to writing screenplays as before and the brothers shared a new common vision of the future. A huge sum of money was invested to build a much larger studio structure including sound-proof air-conditioned sound stages, a laboratory, a cinema hall, and offices and green rooms. The new Basant Studios once again saw the Wadia brothers in the saddle, its imposing twenty-foot-high gates announcing the continuing success of the brothers.

Nonetheless, the heyday of the stunt film was over by 1943. After almost ten years, the Nadia thrill was by and large gone, and the public shrank to a die-hard faithful community of fans. Thanks to the well-developed distribution network at home and abroad, there was still a large enough audience to tide Nadia over the next sixteen years. Up until 1959, she made on an average one, sometimes two films annually. Like *Hunterwali Ki Beti*, these were predominantly remakes of her earlier successes. *Stunt Queen* (1945), *Toofani Tirandaz* (1946), *Comet* (1949), *Sher Dil* (1954) and *Circus Queen* (1959)—to name but a few—were quickly and cheaply produced formula films. Homi Wadia simply used the backdrops of big budget film. As the eternal reincarnation of Hunterwali, Nadia remained a feminist special case in the Indian cinematic world of deities.

9

LET THE WHIP CRACK

Nadia in her trademark costume

6 November 1947 was to be like no other day in Nadia's life. It was the day of Haidee's navjote, the celebration of the initiation rite of the young Parsi. JBH and his wife Hilla had invited Homi and Nadia as a couple to this important celebration—to formally introduce the film star into the family at last. Almost fifty years later, Nadia and Homi told their great-nephew Riyad Wadia what had happened.

As usual, Nadia had got up very early, had completed her extensive morning gymnastics routine and taken a light breakfast. Performing her morning ablutions, she regarded herself for a very long time in the mirror and took a deep breath. As nervous as before a premiere, she did her hair, played distractedly with her dogs and finally applied her make-up with particular care. A few hours later, Homi steered his new Mercedes up Marine Drive to collect Nadia. He was nervous as well, but became somewhat calmer when he entered Nadia's apartment. His love of many years looked charming in her elegant sari with her perfect hairdo and her finely proportioned face. They both tried to dissipate the fear of the other.

In the splendid art deco hall of the Casa da Vinci, the first guests had already gathered, among them Haidee's grandmother, the dowager Dhunmai, and the closest members of the family. JBH greeted his mother warmly and led her into an adjoining room. There he told her that Homi would be taking part in the ceremony accompanied by Nadia. The white-haired old lady looked her son in the eyes and without another word returned to the hall. JBH hadn't dared hope for more. In the reception hall where the ceremony was to take place, the Parsi priest and his six helpers were preparing the sacred fire. The guests kept coming in ever greater numbers. JBH also used the opportunity to emphasize his status as a film mogul, and had invited numerous friends and prominent guests. JBH's star had lost some of its lustre in the years since Nadia's expulsion from the studio, and now he was putting the finishing touches to a big budget film that he hoped would put him back at the top. Starring the upcoming discovery Dilip Kumar with another new star Nargis, this film was based on an original story written by his wife Hilla. JBH had roped in the emerging popular music director Naushad to create an unparalleled musical score and had encouraged debutante director of photography, Fali Mistry to emulate the low-key expressionistic black-and-white photography of Hollywood noir. Titled *Mela*, the film was to premiere soon and Haidee's navjote provided just the social occasion to make the announcement. The film would become the biggest hit of 1948, heralding the 'golden years' of the 1950s, and a revival of J.B.H. Wadia's career as a producer of class films.

The guests were enchanted by the glamorous atmosphere and listened carefully to JBH's words. Soon after the speech, when eager chat about the latest political developments in the newly independent country continued, everyone fell silent again, as though on command: Homi and Nadia came through the door. The well-known star thought for a moment that the floor was shifting under her feet, and Homi visibly paled beneath his brown skin.

It was Hilla of all people who first stepped out of the crowd towards the couple, and with a warm embrace welcomed Nadia. The hatchet was, at that moment, buried once and for all between the two women, and a new era was to begin. Then all eyes turned to Dhunmai who had taken her place on her favourite armchair, looking regal in her white silk sari. Homi and Nadia approached her. The dowager looked penetratingly at Nadia and got up slowly, very slowly, from her chair. Everyone could see how she finally opened her arms to officially accept the famous film star into her family. Nadia's eyes grew moist as Homi bent down to touch his mother's feet in the traditional greeting. The solemn silence was broken by ten-year-old Haidee, who suddenly appeared to let everyone know she was ready for the navjote ceremony. Delighted, and with a new confidence, Nadia mingled with the guests, many of whom she knew. For Haidee and Nadia, the navjote ceremony was an unforgettable occasion.

From Hollywood to Kashmir

Shortly afterwards, Dhunmai suffered a heart attack and was bedridden until her death in 1958. As the more financially successful brother, Homi saw generously to the well-being of his sisters. They were grateful and showed it not least with their demonstration of respect for his private life, something that Homi had long yearned for. Nadia was now part of the family, and as Homi's official partner was a regular at the Wadia house. The couple still lived apart, but they often travelled to the beach hut in Juhu and spent pleasurable weekends there. Quite often they were accompanied by friends. Nadia went swimming regardless of the weather, even if it was raining. She confessed to a friend that she rather liked it as it made Homi pace the beach, nervous and restless. There was also a cook in the beach cottage who didn't serve dinner until around midnight, after the singing, dancing, chatting and games were all over.

Homi and Nadia were obsessed with parlour games, and most of all they liked dressing up. Especially at Christmas, Homi went to extra lengths to surprise his guests—once he appeared on elephant back, dressed as Father Christmas, another time he arrived on camel back, and once in a vintage car.

As for Nadia, she provided her neighbours with a sight for sore eyes almost daily when she walked her five dogs. She always wore shorts on these walks through Colaba; the dogs, however, were clad in pretty little rain capes during the monsoon season. Nadia and her mother were well known in the neighbourhood as an eccentric pair. Nadia was often greeted as 'Hunterwali' by passers-by and her mother too had become a famous local figure. She asked for a little pocket money from Nadia every day which she then immediately sprinkled down in a joyful cascade from her balcony to the beggars on the street. Nadia approved of this. The two shared a very close relationship, and the daughter suffered for a long time when her mother died in 1967. 'As a chain-smoker, Mummy died of lung cancer at the age of eighty-four. But she was nimble to the end and always in good humour.'

Nadia herself had given up smoking in 1951; the doctor had insisted on it because of her asthma. Less successful was her attempt to stop drinking. Time and again there were unpleasant, dramatic scenes under the influence of alcohol. Rather than prevent Nadia from drinking, Homi, who liked a drink himself, preferred to join her. But on the bad nights when Nadia lay unconscious in the bathtub or aggravated common friends with strange phone calls, Homi came to her aid and stayed faithfully by her side right through the hangover.

The couple often went on holiday. Travelling was a shared passion. They travelled whenever the studio allowed, most often by ship to Europe, Australia, Hong Kong or Singapore. One of the loveliest experiences was the visit to Hollywood in 1956. Homi and Nadia had numerous friends in the studios there and were received as guests of honour everywhere they went.

'We had a perfectly splendid time,' Homi recalls with a roguish smile. One evening, they encountered the notorious gossip columnist Louella Parsons. Nadia and Homi's companions grew nervous, for Nadia had on that of all evenings discovered a liking for the diabolical 'Zombie' cocktail and was in an exuberant mood. 'She won't write anything mean about Indian visitors,' Nadia maintained coolly and went right up to the severe reporter. Louella was completely captivated by Nadia's charm and wit, and in her column there was not a negative word to be read.

On this journey, Nadia and Homi made stopovers in England where Bobby was living. Bobby absolutely wanted to be English and from his earliest childhood cherished the desire to follow the call of his nickname and become a London policeman. He had turned down Homi's offer of a partnership in Basant Studios. 'He certainly had the right stature then to be a policeman but he failed the exam,' Homi reports. 'When we arrived, he was working as a postman. That was poison for his health, the damp climate didn't agree with Bobby at all. Though, at the time he looked quite well—probably because he had just fallen in love with a nurse. One month later, he still hadn't recuperated; on the contrary he could hardly walk. We begged him to return to India with us. Finally, he succumbed. We took him with us in a wheelchair! At home he had to climb the steps on all fours. But Nadia took him in hand during the subsequent weeks. Every morning she did gymnastics with him, at first he screamed in pain, but she didn't relent. Incredibly, he recovered so well under Nadia's care that shortly afterwards he took up hockey professionally.'

With the private changes that the 1950s brought for Nadia, her position in the studio changed too. She was addressed respectfully by the employees as 'madam' and regarded as the producer's wife. While she still enjoyed fooling around with colleagues as much as before, she was happy about the privilege of not having to come to the studio every day. She took an active interest in what went on but basically restricted her presence to her own films. Basant Studios and the Wadia brothers found new successes in this period as producers of mythological films and films based on the *Arabian Nights*. Homi innovated with colour, and films like *Hatim Tai*, *Zimbo*, *Zabak*, *Sampoorna Ramayana*, *Ram Bhakta Hanuman* and *Captain Kishore* made millions for the brothers. In 1958, the brothers and Nadia celebrated twenty-five years of film production with a huge party where the entire film industry was invited. Nadia received the lion's share of whistles and applause from the gathered crowd.

Nadia's fifty-second birthday was rapidly approaching and her age was gradually showing in her face and her movements. More and more stunts in her films around this time had to be performed by young male doubles in blonde wigs. She wasn't herself sure how she should make her exit from the film business as long as Homi continued to offer her new roles. He was responsible, she trusted him. Given his predilection for surprises, he turned Nadia's final performance into a spectacle. The Basant team had prepared the mahurat ceremony for a new film on Maundy Thursday. From the backdrop to the obligatory coconut all was ready for the first shot. Nadia arrived at the set punctually, in costume and with an intricate mask when Homi greeted her in front of the entire team: 'You can take off your make-up, let's get married tomorrow!' The Catholic, who had been longing for nothing else so fervently for such a long time, responded: 'Tomorrow is Good Friday, we can't get married then!' Indeed, Homi had hatched up this surprise just the evening before—he didn't want to make the film any more. Suddenly it was crystal clear to him that Nadia should remain blooming and beautiful in the memory of her fans. Enough of the acting!

Nadia was happy. They postponed the wedding date to Easter Sunday. A small celebration took place in Casa da Vinci for the closest circle. Then the newly-weds packed their cases and in a flurry embarked on their honeymoon to Kashmir.

Though bidding adieu to films, Nadia didn't exactly disappear from public life. As the wife of a producer with plenty of free time, she turned her focus of activity to the splendid Bombay racetrack—as a horse breeder. Together with Homi, she spent every Saturday and Sunday on the track where they, as members of the Royal Western India Turf Club, had a box of their own and were regarded as celebrities. This was not only because of the married couple's past in the film business. In 1967, Nadia caused a great stir among the racing-obsessed Bombay society. Her stallion Nijinksi won eight races straightaway, among them the Great Indian Derby. The newspaper reports show Nadia, all in white, at Homi's side, with sunglasses and a content, proud smile of victory which makes her look like the majestic wife of a president.

At that time, Nadia's former acting rival and later friend Madhuri affirms, the atmosphere at the racing course was far more elegant than it is today. Nadia's fantastic parties after the wins, the champagne flowing copiously, remain unforgotten today. 'She was very popular and had lots of friends. I think it was Nadia's friendly and warm-hearted nature that made her so attractive. Her nature was generous, not in the sense of someone who gave presents and whatnot. She had this aura ... she gave a person the feeling that if it came to the crunch she would do anything for you.'

Madhuri, who as 'sweetheart of the north' in the 1930s had felt suffocated by Nadia's successes, is glad today to have been able to forget 'the old competitive story' in the course of time. At the racetrack, a friendship began between the two ex-stars. 'We met often, mostly in society, but oddly we hardly ever talked about our experiences in the film business. Every now and then we would take a peek at old photos all right, and then one would say to the other: "Ah, yes, I remember that film of yours well"—it never went further than that. Nadia didn't miss the work in the studio, she was happily married and it always seemed to me that she was content with her lot.'

Khiladi: Nadia Goes Camp

At the end of the 1960s, Homi's tireless élan as a producer seemed to be waning. He had been in the business for decades, constantly looking for new material and fresh faces to be always a little ahead of the public's taste. He was weary and sucked dry, and this hadn't gone completely unnoticed in the account books of Basant Studios. One employee said to him: 'Boss, let's do another film with Madam ... that will bring good fortune.'

For the second time in the studio's history, Nadia was to see Basant Studios out of a crisis. It was nine years since she had been in front of a camera but the sixty-year-old didn't deliberate for long when Homi offered her the role of a top spy at the side of the charming young man Dileep Raj. *Khiladi* (1968) was the name of this Indian James Bond imitation, a thriller full of wit, panache and grandiose swimming-pool scenes. The steamy, hysterical song-and-dance inserts with playboy costumes or *Raumschiff Orion* (a German *Star Trek*-esque series which attained a cult status) suits alone make *Khiladi* a real find for all fans of 1960s cinema.

Nadia plays 'Madame X1', the grande dame of an organization of government agents. At the start you see her as the target of wild shooting. From all sides enormous guns fire at her simultaneously. Nadia writhes and crumples until she seems to be mortally hit and collapses. The young agents look on, devastated, until Nadia leaps up and with hearty laughter announces: 'Excellent, gentlemen. The experiment with the bullet-proof vest was a success.' She pulls down the zip of her thin jacket and disappears into a garden where numerous young agents are doing acrobatics between the flower beds and practising close combat. Nadia runs from one to the next, giving tips and tricks, delivers an exemplary punch here, chucks a smart young thing over her shoulder there. A little later, the fit senior agent is given her mission. Together with the Indian James Bond, she is to find a professor kidnapped by the terrorist organization Golden Dragon. In the course of his experiments, the professor has developed the formula for a drug that could

Stills from Khiladi, *1968*

destroy the nation, indeed the whole world. It is important to rescue him from the clutches of the Golden Dragon—a life-threatening top-secret task!

The actual mission doesn't appear to unsettle Nadia any more than having a cup of coffee in the morning. Indeed, her handsome partner, the 'Agent 707'—the chief had introduced him on-screen and via radio—makes the matter rather enticing. 'A lover of every sort of beauty,' she comments on his exterior with a knowing laugh. No macho could have reacted with more sangfroid. Even before the titles, Nadia, in her tight, black cocktail dress with pearls and fashionable white stilettos on her feet, establishes a grandiose subversion of the Bond girls. And she keeps it up all through the film. With the use of the most modern technology, the terrorist group is pursued in water, land and air.

Being an agent provides Nadia with the opportunity of serenely producing her repertoire of acting ability. Her codename is 'Living Fireball' and she is considered an expert of disguise. At the airport she pretends to be a Sikh taxi driver with a turban. In a nightclub she mixes cocktails as a moustached bartender. As a curious old man with many physical failings, she gains entrance to an office in order to set up bugs connecting it to her headquarters and, as quick as lightning, to install complicated secret weapons. Her most impressive stunt is as a disguised construction worker on the roof of a skyscraper. She swiftly clambers up a crane and from the control box manages to get her partner to fly across in a concrete tub over the not-yet-finished, new skyline of Bombay.

Khiladi is an entertaining action film which pulls out all the stops. For today's viewer the action seems more amusing than anything else, but that doesn't do the cinema experience any harm. The earnest attempt to keep the audience holding its breath is apparent. Nadia's role in particular, sensitively incorporating her age and her legendary cinema past, lends *Khiladi* an elegant irony. She never falls into the nasty traps set out for older actresses; she never appears as a benevolent granny. Nadia does not make a caricature of Madame X1. She is neither naïve nor asexual. Even in disguise she retains a ladylike dignity, and if there is something to laugh about, it is she herself who laughs the loudest. She plays the agent with plenty of awareness of the funny moments which are inherent when a sixty-year-old fights at the side of a fit beau with the help of helicopters and top secret service technology against an international criminal organization. The tightrope walk she embarks upon under Homi's direction shows, too, that they have both understood 'camp' culture even before Hollywood began to revel with an intellectual joy in kitsch and triviality.

Nadia's final role also suggests that in her advancing years she garnered more and more pleasure in the osmosis between her private life and the world of cinema. That's how Jehangir Modi, a young friend of the family, remembers her as he speaks rapturously about a dinner they had together at the end of the 1970s. Nadia and Homi came two hours late as is the norm in Bombay. She was wearing a skin-tight leopard suit and had well manicured nails, varnished a deep red. That outfit, daring for her age, seemed all the more exotic as Nadia was supporting herself on a crutch because of a hip problem. 'I remember Nadia as a lady who enjoyed making others laugh. That evening she managed to get the entire company creased up with laughter as she told how she had recently taken a tumble on the way to the bathroom.'

At around this time, Nadia also pioneered the Indian fitness wave. In matters of sports and exercises, Nadia was considered quite an expert. She had taken it up when Indian housewives didn't waste a thought on superfluous pounds. Thanks to her, the fitness regimen at which fine ladies had earlier smiled suddenly became very fashionable—the in thing. In various magazines you saw Nadia photographed winking as she performed particular exercises, and she gave interviews about morning gymnastics, calories, eating and sleeping habits. Among others, *Health and Nutrition* asked her: 'Are you satisfied with your weight?'

'Yes, now it's perfect, and the most important curves are still intact. Wouldn't you agree? Homi is satisfied at any rate. I weigh between sixty-one and sixty-three kilograms. Earlier though I weighed eighty kilos. Then Dr R.N. Cooper, my house doctor, recommended the gentlest of all diets to me. I had tried all sorts of drastic programmes and had experienced the yo-yo effect as well. Dr Cooper said: "Simply eat a little less than you actually want to. Of three things, eat only two, from two things, only one. Eat everything—your body needs it!" And gradually I lost weight—and hooray!—I stayed at that weight!'

Darling Edna

Nadia's best friend in those years was Edna. The two had met on a pleasure trip to Hong Kong in 1961 and had become inseparable ever since. Edna was an imposing sight who favoured knee-length pink dresses, an abundance of rubies and diamonds and said 'darling' to everyone. As an Englishwoman in India, Edna cultivated the sort of eccentricity Bombay is famed for. She would slip into paroxysms of delight while narrating tales of her suitors in her early days in Yorkshire. There was an amusing Pole and a Greek who looked like Onassis, and who was, unfortunately, far too old. 'Darling, I didn't miss out on anything!' she insists. Eventually, she married a Sikh who was studying in England: 'My family was horrified that I wanted to marry a coloured person.' But Edna would not be swayed. She learned to cook spicy Indian meals, and as a young mother and wife moved to Bombay in 1959 where she underwent a double culture shock. For the first time in her life she saw people who were too poor to buy shoes. She herself had arrived from the lower middle-class Yorkshire milieu and had ironically moved almost overnight into the elite of Bombay society. 'I do wish someone would write the lively story of my life—under a pseudonym, of course,' she laughs.

It certainly wasn't merely due to their identical hair colour that Edna was often taken for Nadia's younger sister. As extremely zestful Europeans in Bombay, the two were linked by the will to enjoy to the full in their older years all they had missed out on in their youth: being part of a society whose strict etiquette had often humiliated and excluded them when they were young. Edna and Nadia encouraged each other in their determination as wives to call the shots themselves. Edna recounted, for example, the story of a common friend from Punjab who possessed supernatural powers and could contact dead people in séances. According to Edna, this woman was married to a tyrant. Over and over again she came to Bombay to pour her heart out. Nadia and Edna comforted her with warm words, but also with a warm glass of brandy. Once, tipsy, the friend took an unfortunate tumble and broke her arm. Wisely enough, Nadia and Edna explained that the friend had tripped on the stairs thanks to her high-heeled shoes, but the truth came to light. The tyrannical husband took Nadia to task in front of everyone, but she replied with a slap: 'How dare you talk to me in that manner! You are not married to me after all!'

Such troubles were rare, Edna assures. The two of them took care of their image in society with generous donations to church and social institutions. They had a reserved place in the Bombay Gymkhana Club and were accompanied by their husbands to the theatre with perfect old-world charm. On 'jolly' afternoons, the Chinese hairdresser freshened the perms of both ladies at home! And yes, the outings to the harbour were marvellous too. Sunken into Victorian cushioned furniture, surrounded by thousands of ornaments and with a gimlet in a crystal glass, Edna reminisces about the years with Nadia again. Together, the two friends enjoyed a glamorous life of luxury and amusement, as long as they managed to keep the not inconsiderable cliffs and abysses in the exotic world of Bombay at a distance.

The Comeback

February 1993 saw the sixtieth anniversary of Wadia Movietone. Homi started to make plans for the celebration a good half year in advance and intended to screen some of the well-preserved and important Fearless Nadia films once more. With this in mind, he turned to his great-nephew Riyad Wadia who had studied film in Australia and had taken over the reins of Wadia Movietone, producing advertising films and software for television under that banner. Riyad suggested that Homi and Nadia postpone the festival until his documentary film *Fearless—The Hunterwali Story* was complete. It was his first film, a portrait of Nadia and Wadia Movietone, and Riyad had started work on it in 1990 on personal finances. For the premiere, Riyad planned to organize a large festival and was looking for an appropriate place and a sponsor for the event. Homi, however, didn't want to wait. A certain stubbornness made him stick to his original plan and, without informing Riyad, he booked a small cinema for several showings for February 1993. He also thought that Riyad should get a move on. It didn't seem right to him that Riyad work so long on one documentary film—in the same time he had completed entire feature films in the past!

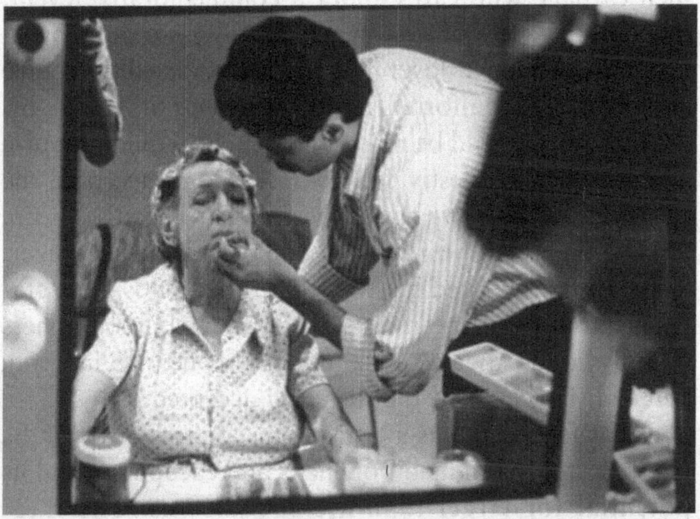

Nadia being made up for Riyad's documentary, 1993

Riyad was hardly delighted about Homi going his own way. He was also under pressure, for the work on the Nadia film was turning out to be more complicated than he had imagined. The abundance of film copies, the partially and badly damaged negatives, the programmes, newspaper articles, photos were spread over diverse offices, sitting rooms and cellars. Some were also in the film archive in Pune. The majority of these dusty treasures were packed away in a number of enormous boxes. Sorting through the material was a task worthy of Sisyphus. The closer Homi's planned festival came, the clearer it was that Riyad couldn't get his film ready in time.

In January 1993, Bombay erupted with violent communal riots in the wake of the destruction of the Babri Masjid. As the city went up in flames and civil-war-like conditions held sway, Homi had to cancel the festival. In the face of such carnage who cares about a commemorative event, especially as stars of yesteryears hardly hold any appeal to the average movie lover in India. Riyad visited the couple in Colaba and comforted them. At the end of March, his documentary would be ready and then he would organize a really nice, big festival. This time Homi accepted the suggestion gratefully, but suggested that Riyad's cousin, Shiamak Davar, be taken on board as co-organizer. Shiamak had worked his way up in the 1980s from star dancer to one of the most sought-after choreographers in Bollywood. Always quick to pick up on a media trend, Shiamak Davar liked the idea and accepted.

What followed was a typical episode from the Wadia family history with its bit of chaos and cacophony and its potential for larger-than-life showdowns. The three individuals, Homi, Shiamak and Riyad had completely different visions of the event, and each of them pressed in a different direction. For his planned *Hunterwali Ballet*, Shiamak Davar had managed to rope in the whiskey label Directors Special as a sponsor, but the marketing experts thought a documentary film the most boring thing in the world. This brought Riyad to the edge of a breakdown, because for him, of course, his film stood as the central point of the festival. And the copy of his first work was still not really ready to be shown, although the advertising campaign had long since begun.

In spite—or because—of the turbulence in the preparation, journalists started to grow interested in the spectacle. Bombay's film critics searched out Nadia in Colaba, asked for interviews and comments on the documentary film which she hadn't yet seen at that point. The event took off: propelled by curiosity and rumours, the cultural pages suddenly discovered an interest in their own film history—normally a terribly neglected subject. In page-long eulogies, Fearless Nadia was heaped with compliments, depicted as 'the Sultana of the stunt genre' and honoured as the first real feminist in Indian cinema, who fifty years ago was more revolutionary than today's youth.

The media hype of the Fearless Nadia Film Festival showed its effect at the opening event on 17 May 1993. The rented cinema with its 700 seats was completely sold out for the screening of *Diamond Queen*. But it was immediately apparent that this public differed from the circle that usually attended film premieres or cultural events. The majority of the filmgoers were white-haired and obviously old. But many of the elderly ladies and gentlemen were accompanied by their grandchildren. When the lights went down and the familiar Wadia ship was seen on the screen, the younger people in the audience were more than a little surprised at the way their grandfathers and grandmothers perked up. Whistles and thunderous applause went through the hall at the first sight of Nadia—blonde, bold and self-confident—on the screen after such a long time.

At this first screening, Homi and Nadia had slipped unnoticed into the crowd, as nervous as they had been at the premiere of *Hunterwali*. How would the public react after all these years? The re-screening of *Diamond Queen* was a wonderful experience for the two of them. It was as though a long-cherished dream was being fulfilled. At the end of the showing, Nadia was, of course, discovered and surrounded by her fans, old and new, who made a beeline for autographs. On the four subsequent evenings, the spectacle repeated itself when *Miss Frontier Mail*, *Muqabala*, *Eleven O'Clock* and *Baghdad Ka Jadoo* were shown.

It was Saturday at last, the day of the premiere of Riyad's documentary, the day of the official commemoration, for which Shiamak Davar's ballet was also billed. In the afternoon, the three main parties in the event admitted that each had taken the initiative to ask his own guests: Homi estimated the number of Nadia and his guests to be around 300, Shiamak had invited 800 people and Riyad 700! By five o'clock in the afternoon, the results could be seen on the streets. The crowd in front of the auditorium swelled so much that the street was blocked—and the police arrived. When it became clear that not even half of the crowd would fit into the hall, a fight broke out—everyone wanted to see Fearless Nadia, some had travelled especially from Pune, others had been waiting in line for hours. Riyad tried to intervene, with the result that he was dragged into the throng and was at the receiving end of a couple of powerful punches. Just before his new suit was torn to shreds, he fled to the theatre, in tears. There, Nadia, Homi, the prominent guests of honour and the general audience in the overflowing auditorium were wondering why the lights were still not being dimmed! Riyad hurriedly dusted himself down, went to the stage with trembling knees and, illuminated by old Wadia Movietone spotlights, gave a short speech in Nadia's honour. He dedicated the evening to his deceased grandfather J.B.H. Wadia—and the show began.

With verve, wit and charm, *Fearless—The Hunterwali Story* portrayed Nadia's screen career. And everyone in the public who thought that Indian film history was a tiresome business, better left to cinema experts, was caught up in the daring stunts and the flair of a time when film-making had more to do with adventures than with the producers' greed for money. Whoever hadn't known before, understood in the following sixty minutes what a wonderfully brave, witty actress Nadia was. Fate must have been in a festive mood when she led Nadia to the Wadia brothers where it all began.

The applause didn't abate! Everyone rose to their feet in ovation when Nadia finally came to the stage. It grew perfectly still as she went to the microphone. But overcome with emotion she couldn't speak. This time the public didn't mind her tears—on the contrary, everyone in the public seemed infected by the emotion of this woman who had never before been so honoured. Sobbing, Nadia thanked her fans for their support and loyalty through the decades of her long career. Her eyes fixed on Homi, she thanked him for his love. Finally, she thanked her great-nephew Riyad for bringing all the lovely memories back to life.

To thunderous applause she finally left the stage and handed it over to the *Hunterwali Ballet*, choreographed in her honour. For a full hour, Shiamak Davar's enormous ensemble danced and leaped in Fearless Nadia costumes across the stage. The mist rose, the whips cracked, and calls of 'He-y-y-y!' rent the air. It was a grand epilogue for the evening during which Nadia was officially accepted into the circle of the great Indian cinema legends. After a few glasses of champagne, Homi and Nadia floated on a wave of triumph back to Colaba, long past midnight.

Riyad Wadia needed a holiday after the strenuous time. He travelled to Europe. In his luggage he had several cassettes of his Nadia film which he handed over at the offices of various film festivals, among them London and Berlin. The tour with *Fearless—The Hunterwali Story* began in 1994, taking Riyad round the world several times. Wherever the film was shown, the cinema audience gaped at the blonde actress from India. They were enchanted and amazed, and there were always some individuals who asked whether the story was really true. And how was it possible that nothing had ever been heard of these films? Nadia herself could no longer travel, but she listened to detailed reports from Riyad after each festival, smiling and content. Most of all, she was delighted to learn that in spite of the many clips, people could scarcely believe that films like these were made in India so long ago. At one point, however, shortly before her death, it was Nadia who put a question to her great-nephew: was it really true that Hollywood was considering making a film on her life?

Nadia died on 9 January 1996, a day after her birthday, as a result of a heart attack. Ever since, Homi has paid regular visits to her grave and perfumed the dark marble stone.

EPILOGUE: LADIES' LUNCH

Ladies' Lunch is a weekly ritual that has been retained beyond Nadia's death. Every Friday at lunchtime, Nadia's women friends, an illustrious gathering of elderly ladies, meet in her old-fashioned apartment. With its hundreds of old film posters, awards, photos and paper cuttings, Nadia's home has become a small museum in which Homi keeps the memory of his wife alive in a moving, almost jealous manner. The old furniture, the small Nadia altar on the television, the wobbly table with the telephone and the deep, sunken armchairs—everything is just as she left it. Homi recounts that in the first weeks after Nadia's funeral none of the ladies came. But they kept calling and saying how much they missed Nadia. Until Edna eventually asked if they could continue the tradition for Nadia's sake—a wish that Homi was glad to consent to. For thirty-six years, the charmer has played the role of the cock among the hens at the ladies' lunch.

As a greeting, Edna tells how her daughter in England is filing for divorce and that this story is upsetting her almost as much as when Indira Gandhi's aunt's corpse had to be transported to India from England, and her wig went missing in the process and how Edna had to keep the deceased fresh with ice cubes on her last voyage. She rings the bell for Homi's servant and has her glass generously filled with brandy; the sticker on the bottle is labelled 'Madam Edna' in black. Then she unpacks the stepper, a handy sport machine for senior citizens. In the afternoon heat, she demonstrates to the circle how practical, simple and effective the machine is. One after the other, all present have to try out the stepper and are told how in addition one ought to do some gymnastic exercises in bed in the morning, drink a large glass of water, and how that effectively gets rid of 'all poisons in the body'.

The ladies' circle is delighted when Varuna comes through the door. Some years ago she had moved to Pune with her husband and she therefore makes it to the Ladies' Lunch only once in a while. Nadia enjoyed a close friendship with the elegant lady, the origins of which are recalled on this visit. Varuna grew up as a Bengali princess, had played with tiger cubs in her father's palace, and her every wish was fulfilled. Only the cinema was somewhat taboo for her, but it was precisely this that exerted an attraction on the princess again and again. She bunked school, especially when Nadia films were showing. Decades later, in the exclusive Bombay Gymkhana Club, Varuna saw a blonde lady standing at the bar—and all the excitement of those days came rushing back. 'Then I did something that my husband found impossible, because it's impolite and contrary to all etiquette. I went right up to the lady and asked: "Are you not Hunterwali?" Nadia was very pleased and said: "Oh, you remember! Did you like the film?" Then she embraced me and invited me to have a drink. At that time I didn't even know Nadia's real name. She introduced me to Homi, I fetched my husband and we became good friends.' Varuna, Edna, Nadia and their husbands formed a cosy, well-knit group in the subsequent years, spending one weekend in Edna's country house, the next with Homi and Nadia at Juhu Beach, and during the week they met at the Gymkhana Club in the evenings for dinner and dance or a game of cards.

The hours at the Ladies' Lunch gently pass accompanied by sweet wine. Homi recounts his trip to Egypt and how upon his return he had received love letters from a belly-dancer and how Nadia was terribly jealous about that. Egypt was quite wonderful, but nonetheless the eighty-eight-year old has another destination in mind for his next journey, Kathmandu. One of the ladies would prefer Australia, the next South Africa. And Edna: 'I've been everywhere already, I would prefer to simply stay put in Bombay and, more precisely, in the Geoffrey Bar. But my husband only lets me out during the day, he is so terribly jealous.' At some point, around four o'clock in the afternoon, lunch is finally served in the kitchen, and a little later the amusingly tipsy ladies trip on their way, until next Friday.

FILMOGRAPHY*

1933	Lal-e-Yaman	Wadia Movietone/Wadia Brothers
1934	Noor-e-Yaman	Wadia Movietone/Wadia Brothers
	Desh Deepak	Wadia Movietone/Wadia Brothers
1935	Hunterwali	Wadia Movietone/Wadia Brothers
1936	Pahadi Kanya	Wadia Movietone/Wadia Brothers
	Miss Frontier Mail	Wadia Movietone/Wadia Brothers
1937	Hurricane Hansa	Wadia Movietone/Wadia Brothers
1938	Lutaru Lalna	Wadia Movietone/Wadia Brothers
1939	Punjab Mail	Wadia Movietone/Wadia Brothers
1940	Diamond Queen	Wadia Movietone/Wadia Brothers
1941	Bambaiwali	Wadia Movietone/Wadia Brothers
1942	Jungle Princess	Wadia Movietone/Wadia Brothers
	Muqabala	Wadia Movietone/Wadia Brothers
	Mouj	Basant Pictures/Wadia Brothers
1943	Hunterwali Ki Beti	Basant Pictures/Wadia Brothers
1945	Sher-e-Baghdad	Basant Pictures/Wadia Brothers
	Flying Prince	Basant Pictures/Wadia Brothers
	Stunt Queen	Basant Pictures/Wadia Brothers
	Himmatwali	Nanabhai Bhatt/Wadia Brothers
1946	Toofani Tirandaz	Basant Pictures/Wadia Brothers
	Lady Robin Hood	Nanabhai Bhatt/Wadia Brothers
	Mohabbat Ki Jeet	Ramjibhai Thakur/Wadia Brothers

* Refer www.wadiamovietone.com for more information.

1947	Eleven O'Clock	Basant Pictures/Wadia Brothers
	Tigress	Basant Pictures/Wadia Brothers
	Toofan Queen	Nanabhai Bhatt/Wadia Brothers
	Chabuk Sawar	Super Pictures/Wadia Brothers
1948	Maya Mahal	Basant Pictures/Wadia Brothers
	Jungle Goddess	Super Pictures/Wadia Brothers
	Kismatwale	RMV Productions/Wadia Brothers
1949	Comet	Basant Pictures/Wadia Brothers
	Delhi Express	Nanabhai Bhatt/Wadia Brothers
	Billi/The Wild Cat	Super Pictures/Wadia Brothers
1950	Circuswale	Basant Pictures/Wadia Brothers
1952	Jungle Ka Jawahar	Basant Pictures/Wadia Brothers
1954	Sher Dil	Basant Pictures/Wadia Brothers
1955	Carnival Queen	Basant Pictures/Wadia Brothers
1956	Baghdad Ka Jadoo	Basant Pictures/Wadia Brothers
	Fighting Queen	Pramila Kumar/Wadia Brothers
1957	Diler Daku	Basant Pictures/Wadia Brothers
1959	Circus Queen	Basant Pictures/Wadia Brothers
1968	Khiladi	Basant Pictures/Wadia Brothers
1993	Fearless—The Hunterwali Story	Riyad Vinci Wadia/Wadia Movietone Pvt. Ltd.

ACKNOWLEDGEMENTS

For the warm and informative companionship during my research I want to give special thanks to Riyad Wadia. Many thanks also to the other members of the Wadia family, in particular Homi and Haidee, as well as Edna Nair, Uma da Cunha, Suresh Chabria, P.K. Nair, Neela Karnik, Khanderao Kelkar, Firoze Rangoonwalla, Janet Fine, Jehangir Modi, Esther Abraham, Beryl Doyley, Ismail Shaikh, Shiv and Varuna Rathore, Nanabhai Bhatt, Babubhai Mistri, Biplab Basu, Margret Plath, Barbara Wenner, Helmut Höge, Diana Zimmermann, Hella Knappertsbusch, Matthias Landwehr, Holger Kuntze, Erika and Ulrich Gregor, Marian Stefanowski, and the people at the Friends of the German Cinematheque, the International Forum of Young Film, Berlin, as well as the National Film Archive, Pune, and to Karthika and Shantanu at Penguin Books India.